GLOBAL GOVERNANCE

Giving the UN the Tools it Needs to Save The World

By Patrick Goggins

Independently published in

Hollywood, Florida

© 2019, Patrick Goggins

ISBN: 9781090891419

All rights reserved. No part of this book may be reproduced in any form or by any electronic or mechanical means, including information storage and retrieval system, without permission in writing from the publisher, except by a reviewer who may quote brief passages in a review.

Contents

I. ABSTRACT --------------------------------------- 1
II. DESCRIPTION OF THE MODEL ------------- 11
NEW POWER AND PURPOSE-------------------- 11
Entry Pact--- 13
Transition -- 13
SEVEN ORGANS --------------------------------- 15
General Assembly ------------------------------- 15
    Composition --------------------------------- 16
    Functions-------------------------------------- 17
    Checks and Balances ---------------------- 18
Security Council -------------------------------- 19
    Composition --------------------------------- 19
    Functions-------------------------------------- 20
    Checks and Balances ---------------------- 21
Economic and Social Council -------------------- 22
    Composition --------------------------------- 23
    Functions-------------------------------------- 23
    Checks and Balances ---------------------- 24
International Court of Justice ------------------- 25
    Composition --------------------------------- 25
    Functions-------------------------------------- 26
    Checks and Balances ---------------------- 26
Secretariat -- 26
    Composition --------------------------------- 27

- Functions --- 28
- Checks and Balances --- 28
- Council of Philosophers and Scientists --- 29
  - Composition --- 29
  - Functions --- 30
  - Checks and Balances --- 31
- World Central Reserve Bank --- 31
  - Composition --- 31
  - Functions --- 32
  - Checks and Balances --- 33
- MANAGING CURRENT AND EMERGING CHALLENGES AND RISKS --- 34
- Reasonable Controls on Capital --- 34
  - Cadaster --- 36
  - Progressive Tax on Capital --- 38
  - Progressive Tax on Income --- 40
  - Limits on Intellectual Property Rights --- 40
  - Global Economic Justice Factor --- 41
  - Limits on Corporate Participation in Elections --- 43
- Social Utility Index --- 43
- The Big Three --- 45
- Genocide and Ethnic Cleansing --- 45

Military Spending ------------------------------ 46
Intelligence Agencies ---------------------------- 47
International Military and Economic Agreements
-- 48
Travel and Naturalization ------------------------ 48
Home Rule/Indigenous Persons ---------------- 49
Political Parties ---------------------------------- 51
Term Limits ------------------------------------- 52
Public Records and Meetings -------------------- 53
Single Subject Limitation ------------------------ 54
Standard Pitch ---------------------------------- 55
III. ARGUMENT --------------------------------- 57
Core Values -------------------------------------- 58
Social Utility ------------------------------------ 58
Definite Values ---------------------------------- 59
Decision-Making Capacity ---------------------- 59
Effectiveness ------------------------------------- 61
Resources and Financing ------------------------ 62
    Human Resources ----------------------------- 63

    Material Resources --------------------------- 63

Trust and Insight -------------------------------- 64
    Trust -- 66

    Insight -- 66

Appointments ----------------------------------- 68

Actions -- 69
Flexibility -- 69
Protection against the Abuse of Power --------- 70
Accountability --------------------------------------- 72
    Performance ------------------------------------- 73

    Accountability ----------------------------------- 73

IV. CONCLUSION --------------------------------- 75
Appendix I --- 79
CHAPTER I: PURPOSES AND PRINCIPLES - 81
CHAPTER II: MEMBERSHIP--------------------- 85
CHAPTER III: ORGANS -------------------------- 89
CHAPTER IV: THE GENERAL ASSEMBLY--- 92
CHAPTER V: THE SECURITY COUNCIL ---- 111
CHAPTER VI: PACIFIC SETTLEMENT OF DISPUTES --- 119
CHAPTER VII: INTERNATIONAL MILITARY INTERVENTION -------------------------------- 123
CHAPTER VIII: REGIONAL MILITARY AGREEMENTS---------------------------------- 132
CHAPTER IX: REGIONAL ECONOMIC AND SOCIAL AGREEMENTS ------------------------- 134
CHAPTER X: THE ECONOMIC AND SOCIAL COUNCIL-- 139
CHAPTER XI: DECLARATION REGARDING COLONIES AND INDIGENOUS PERSONS -- 146

CHAPTER XII: COUNCIL OF PHILOSOPHERS
AND SCIENTISTS --------------------------------- 150

CHAPTER XII: WORLD CENTRAL RESERVE
BANK -- 152

CHAPTER XIV: THE INTERNATIONAL COURT
OF JUSTICE -- 155

CHAPTER XV: THE SECRETARIAT ----------- 160

CHAPTER XVI: MISCELLANEOUS PROVISIONS
--- 166

CHAPTER XVII: NOT USED --------------------- 168

CHAPTER XVIII: AMENDMENTS ------------- 168

CHAPTER XIX: RATIFICATION AND
SIGNATURE --------------------------------------- 169

GLOBAL GOVERNANCE

> "[O]ur aim in founding the State was not the disproportionate happiness of any one class, but the greatest happiness of the whole; we thought that in a State which is ordered with a view to the good of the whole we should be most likely to find justice."
>
> Plato, The Republic

I. ABSTRACT

The world is faced with two imminent existential threats: nuclear weapons, and climate change. They are existential threats because, one, either could end all life on the planet, and two, we currently do not have the political mechanism to control them.

But they can be controlled.

After World War II, the world, sickened by the needless death of millions, the waste of time, energy, and property, and the horror of the thought of it happening again, chose to come together and form the United Nations.

The organization has largely succeeded in achieving its stated goal, listed in the preamble, "to save succeeding generations from the scourge of war," at least to the extent that there hasn't been a global war since.

But we still have war, and we still have nuclear weapons. Like the U.S. Constitution failed to address slavery, the U.N. Charter failed to address nuclear weapons. As of today, there are approximately 15,000 nuclear warheads on the planet, held by eight nation-states. Their collective explosive power, if deployed, would terminate all life on this planet.

In 1945, we only had the slightest idea that our massive consumption of fossil fuels was creating significant amounts of carbon dioxide, and that a shift in the amount of carbon dioxide could have an effect on the planet's climate. Today, not only do we know that the consumption of fossil fuels have an effect on the planet's climate, and that the climate is in fact changing, but that we have only a short time to reverse our dependence on fossil fuels, before climate change becomes both permanent and catastrophic.

The nations of the world have attempted to regulate nuclear weapons and climate change through treaties, but treaties are ineffective,

Global Governance

because compliance is entirely voluntary. This situation was faced before, by the United States of America.

The American experiment began with the Declaration of Independence in 1776. It was soon followed by the Articles of Confederation, which soon proved to be ineffective, as they gave the federal government little power, that is, state compliance with federal law was entirely voluntary. In April 1787, James Madison called the Articles of Confederation "nothing more than a treaty of amity of commerce and of alliance."

The founding fathers' answer was the United States' Constitution, which is arguably a highwater mark of the Enlightenment. It balanced political power among the states and three branches of government and stands today as a model form of national governance.

Still, it is not enough. A third problem faces today's world: economic inequality. It is a systemic problem, in that capitalism is not bound by national borders, and quickly flees to the cheapest place to manufacture goods, which are inevitably the least (and worst) regulated markets. While the U.S. Constitution succeeds in balancing political power, it fails in balancing the power of the people against the economic power of private capital. In the U.S., it's almost as if human rights are contingent while property rights have become absolute. Internationally, the nation-state's very existence is being challenged by the multinational corporation. For instance, under the Trans-Pacific Partnership, nation-states cede sovereignty to arbitration panels composed of international lawyers, allowing multi-national corporations to collect damages from a nation-state, if its laws are enforced in an "arbitrary or unjustifiable manner" or if they "materially impair" the corporation's property rights.[1]

Multi-national corporations, and the billionaires who disproportionately own them, are

---

[1] TPP, Sec. 28.3.1(c)

Global Governance

quickly seizing control of the world economy, at the expense of nearly everyone else. Thomas Picketty's work brings into sharp focus today's destabilizing level of economic inequality. In addition, the alarming willingness of nation-states to cede sovereignty to multi-national corporations can lead to only one result: oligarchy. Like communism and fascism, oligarchy is an extremely imbalanced form of governance, and will result in misery and poverty across the planet.

What can be done to reverse this alarming trend? What can be done to eliminate nuclear weapons and regulate economic activity sufficiently to address climate change? The answer is quite obvious: the United Nations Charter must be amended to give it the power to pass binding laws. It must be able to set global policy, and have the enforcement mechanisms to see that policy is implemented.

The question is one of governance. The nation-state can only pass laws that apply within its borders. It is not in any nation-state's interest to voluntarily surrender the capability to manufacture nuclear weapons, when another nation-state has not done so. Likewise, why would a country put itself at an economic disadvantage with other countries, by adopting strict measures to curb climate change? Remarkably, some countries are doing just that, but their efforts could never be sufficient to adequately address the problem.

The world needs good governance. The first principle of a well-designed governance system is that economic power and political power must be in balance. Under the current system, political power ends at the border. Economic power knows know borders. This gives economic power an advantage, and capitalists are using this advantage to undermine national sovereignty.

The obvious answer is to strengthen international political power, by strengthening the United Nations. Just as the Articles of Confederation were insufficient to govern the early United States, the present United Nations

Global Governance

Charter is insufficient to advance its own goals. It is insufficient because, by design, the U.N. lacks jurisdiction. It is, in Madison's words, a treaty of amity, which leaves the parties mistrustful of the willing compliance of the other parties.

This *Integrated System of International Governance with Limited Jurisdiction* (the "Model") is an amendment to the 1945 U.N. Charter, which can be adopted and ratified by a two-thirds vote of Members and their governments under Article XVIII of the existing Charter, including all of the permanent members of the security council. In the likely event that at least one of the P-5 vetoes the amendment, the remaining Members would be free to re-incorporate the United Nations under an amended Charter, leaving the objecting P-5 members behind.

The Model appears below in Appendix I.

Patrick Goggins

The Model works because it gives the United Nations the jurisdiction to pass and enforce laws in twelve limited areas pertaining to international relations. It draws on the strengths of the U.S. Constitution, and applies concepts of human rights and property rights developed in the Enlightenment and refined through the present day. It is based on structural checks and balances of political and economic power, with an operative emphasis on Jeremy Bentham's theory of social utility.

In addition, the Model includes an all-of-the-above set of good governance features, gleaned from nearly two and a half centuries of experience under the American model.

The global union is strengthened by an entry pact, where Members agree to refrain from conducting most commerce with non-members. The likely Balkanization would be offset by membership and self-sufficiency. In effect, the Model would cause minimal disruption to nation-state sovereignty. Its main feature is

Global Governance

that it eliminates most of the corrupting influences of global capitalism in its current form, while preserving capitalism's best features: innovation and efficiency.

It is the last word in good governance? Absolutely not. It would benefit from input from academics, policy makers, and diplomats. The Model is based largely on the United States' Constitution, which the author is familiar. Another fruitful post-selection endeavor would be to study and integrate the constitutions of the world into the Model. A final unaccomplished task would be a review of the Universal Declaration of Human Rights, omitted from the Model as presented, because it does not involve governance, but under the Model, grants substantive rights.

Patrick Goggins

II. DESCRIPTION OF THE MODEL

NEW POWER AND PURPOSE

The United Nations under the 1945 Charter is largely an advisory body, founded on "faith in fundamental human rights." (Preamble) The General Assembly, for instance, can only "discuss" and "make recommendations to the Members." (Article 10) The Security Council is the most powerful organ under the 1945 Charter, and the five permanent members effectively control the organization. Its four purposes are laudable, but limited. They seek: "To maintain international peace and security... [t]o develop friendly relations among nations," and to "achieve international co-operation." (Article 1)

A concrete example of how the United Nations' limited powers has proven ineffective is the well-meaning, but likely ineffective Paris Accords on climate change. Without the power to compel its members to comply with these agreements, or indeed the power to impose its own regulations, the United Nations is what Thomas G. Weiss and Ramesh Thakur called "global governance without global government." (Weiss, 2010).

The Model adds new power and purpose to the United Nations. It expands existing powers, and gives it new, but limited, legislative, executive, and judicial powers. Power is shifted from the Security Council, which is the only organ authorized to issue binding resolutions under the 1945 Charter, to the General Assembly, which under the Model is vested with the power to legislate.

The United Nation's purpose under the Model is to transition from governance to government. Giving the United Nations real power, albeit limited to specific areas, would allow the organization to effectively manage current and emerging challenges facing our world.

Global Governance

Entry Pact

While the Model gives the seven organs of the United Nations important new powers and purposes, the core of the union is the entry pact, where Members agree that they will do no commerce of any kind with non-member nations, including persons and entities under the non-member's jurisdiction. The sole exception is personal use expenses for travel by Member citizens to non-Member countries, or by non-Member citizens to Member countries.

Transition

The Model involves no constitutional changes to the adopting Members, although certain national laws may have to be changed in order to conform with the amended Charter.

Upon ratification of the Amendment, cash and personal property owned by non-Member citizens in Member countries would be returned to the non-Member citizens. Real property owned by non-Member citizens in Member countries would be sold to Member citizens, and the proceeds returned to the non-Member citizen. Thereafter, property owned by non-Member citizens will be treated as set forth in the articles regarding suspension and expulsion, which are significantly harsher.

Member nations can be suspended, and economic sanctions can be imposed, including seizure of assets. Members can also be expelled, and their assets forfeited, along with the assets of persons and entities under their jurisdiction. Doing business with a non-member is itself grounds for suspension and expulsion. Thus, the economic bond between nations becomes the glue that keeps them united.

Admittedly, this entry pact will result in a certain amount of Balkanization of the United Nations *vis-à-vis* non-Member nations. This actually serves two important purposes: One, it promotes self-sufficiency among the United Nations, while eliminating the corrupting influence of foreign capital. Two, it provides a strong incentive for non-Member nations to become Members. The more nations that join in the United Nations under the Model, the stronger the union. The stronger the union, the more benefits inure to the people living in it.

SEVEN ORGANS

There are seven organs of the United Nations under the Model. The seven organs are given limited powers under the Charter. The existing Trusteeship Council is eliminated because it has fulfilled its purpose; the trusteeship nations, taken from the Axis Powers, have all now achieved home rule. The Model adds two new organs: a Council of Philosophers and Scientists, and a World Central Reserve Bank.

General Assembly

With new legislative powers, the General Assembly becomes the primary agent of change under the Model. Its composition balances the interests of the people and the Member states. Its function is to pass laws that advance the interests of all people, while acting as a counterweight to the economic power of capital.

Composition

Under the Model, the General Assembly is expanded to two houses: the People's Assembly, and the Senate. The people are represented in the People's Assembly by a proportional number of 1,000 total Representatives, based on the Member's population, with not less than 1 or more than 100 Representatives, elected by a popular vote of the people. Representatives are limited to one 7-year term. Members are represented in the Senate by one Senator per Member, appointed by the Member government. Senators are limited to one 14-year term.

Global Governance

Functions

The General Assembly is given legislative power, that is, the power to make laws in twelve enumerated areas. These laws are binding on the Members, as well as the people and legal entities within the Members' jurisdiction. The General Assembly also has nominative functions, and responsibility for the census and cadaster, described below. The jurisdiction of the General Assembly is limited to passing laws in the following areas:

- Progressive taxes on income and capital;

- Debt and a single currency;

- International commerce;

- Relations with non-members;

- Travel, migration, and issue one global passport;

- Limited intellectual property rights;

- Tribunals inferior to the International Court of Justice, specialized agencies and NGOs;

- Pollution and the environment;

- Labor;

- Military and nuclear weapons;

- Limited sovereign jurisdiction over international waters, space, colonies, and Antarctica;

- Laws necessary and proper to execute foregoing powers.

Checks and Balances

Before a bill can be voted on, it must be assigned a social utility rating by the Council of Philosophers and Scientists, this is to give the senators and representatives practical advice, and to make public the social effects of proposed laws. Bills must be voted on in identical forms by both houses before they can become law, and can only embrace one subject. Bills passed by both houses are presented to the Secretary-General, who can either sign or veto the bill. A veto can be over-ridden by a two-thirds majority of each house. Political parties are given non-recognition under the Model, described below.

Security Council

The main innovations to the Security Council under the Model is eliminating the P-5 seats, adding jurisdiction over regional military agreements, the power to direct military action, and enhanced ability to regulate armaments, giving it real power to control the world's nations' ability to conduct war.

Composition

Eliminating the notion of permanent membership, the Security Council is still composed of fifteen members.

Seven members are appointed by a majority of both houses of the General Assembly, who would have a seven-year term. Five members are appointed by the Secretary-General, whose terms would be co-terminus with the Secretary-General. Three members are appointed by the Council of Philosophers and Scientists, who would have a fourteen-year term. No member could have successive terms on the Security Council. The Military Staff Committee is also revitalized under the Model.

Functions

The Security Council would continue to be the world's clearing house for information on armaments and military capability, and under the Model, it has enhanced regulatory authority. The Security Council also would have the power to enforce regional military agreements, and enhanced command

Global Governance

and control authority, with the power to compel Members to commence or cease military operations. It would maintain its role in Chapter VI regarding the pacific settlement of disputes. Chapter VII, Article 41 contains a revised process by which non-military measures would be adopted and implemented. Article 42 provides a revised process by which military measures would be adopted and implemented.

Checks and Balances

The United Nations would have no standing military under the Model. Any military measures would be taken by the Members, under the Security Council's direction. Article 41 provides that the General Assembly must approve proposed non-military intervention by a majority of both houses. To approve military intervention, Article 42 requires two-thirds passage by both houses of the General Assembly, or a determination of emergency by the Secretary-General, which can either be confirmed or dis-authorized by two-thirds of both houses of the General Assembly. Any authorization for military action can be revoked or nullified by unanimous vote of the Council of Philosophers and Scientists. Members can dispute the Security Council's military directives to the Secretary-General, and are subject to suspension or expulsion for failing to comply with valid military directives.

Economic and Social Council

The Economic and Social Council is reduced in size in the Model – from fifty-four seats to forty-two. It would be given new powers regarding regional economic agreements and the cadaster, discussed below, and its existing powers in relation to the specialized agencies would be expanded.

Composition

The Economic and Social Council consists of forty-two Members of the United Nations. Twenty-one members would be appointed by the General Assembly, fourteen members by the Secretary General, seven Members by the Council of Philosophers and Scientists. Members have a term of three years, with one third of the seats being re-appointed each year. There would be no term limit.

Functions

The Economic and Social Council would have primary authority over regional economic agreements, and the lead in a process to bring the specialized agencies and non-governmental organizations into the United Nations.

It would be primarily responsible to perform the cadaster and the census, described below, with the power to compel and enjoin Members, as well as persons, and entities under their jurisdiction, to provide the necessary data for the cadaster. Lastly, it would be required to make an annual report to the General Assembly and the Secretary-General on global economic inequality.

Checks and Balances

Because its functions are mostly ministerial, there are few structural balances on the Economic and Social Council in the Model, except for the right to appeal certain directives to the Secretary-General, and then the International Court of Justice.

Global Governance

International Court of Justice

The size of the Court remains the same under the Model, but the selection process is improved, judicial terms are for life instead of nine years. Its decisions now have the force of law, whereas under the 1945 Charter, each Member "undertakes to comply" with the decisions of the Court. (Article 94.1)

Composition

The International Court of Justice would be composed of fifteen judges, nominated by the Secretary-General, and confirmed by two-thirds of the Senate. They would hold office during good behavior – meaning for life, unless impeached. The General Assembly could create inferior courts, which judges are appointed and hold terms like the International Court of Justice.

Functions

The International Court of Justice would be given judicial power, that is, the power to issue binding decisions on a limited range of cases and controversies, mainly those arising under the Charter or the laws of the United Nations. Members that fail to comply with orders of the International Court of Justice would be subject to sanctions, suspension, and expulsion.

Checks and Balances

Criminal cases would be decided by jury. Judges would be subject to impeachment for high crimes and abuse of office.

Secretariat

The Model changes how the Secretary-General is appointed, and adds an International Space and Maritime Commission to the secretariat,

Global Governance

which would administer the United Nations' sovereign jurisdiction over colonies, international waters, Antarctica, and outer space.

Composition

The Secretary-General would be nominated by either the Security Council, the Economic and Social Council, or the Council of Philosophers and Scientists, and elected by a two-thirds vote of both houses of the General Assembly. The Secretary-General would be limited to one seven-year term in office. In the event the Secretary-General dies or becomes incapacitated, the chair of the Council of Philosophers and Scientists would hold the executive power *pro tem*, until such time as the General Assembly can elect a new Secretary-General. The secretariat is composed of permanent staffs assigned to the organs of the United Nations.

Patrick Goggins

Functions

The Secretary-General would be given executive power, that is, the power to execute laws duly enacted by the General Assembly. There would also be a wide array of ministerial duties, scattered throughout the Model. The Secretary-General would also be tasked with proposing to the General Assembly, a code of ethics, which will govern conflicts of interest and abuse of office in the United Nations.

Checks and Balances

The Secretary-General could be impeached for high crimes and abuse of office. The Model also provides expanded anti-discrimination language, and for a code of ethics which makes termination for abuse of office mandatory by staff, and if it is a Charter-level office, grounds for impeachment.

Global Governance

Council of Philosophers and Scientists

The Council of Philosophers and Scientists is an innovation under the Model. Its primary function is to focus the United Nations on social utility, so that the United Nations can maximize the benefits of its actions. The council also provides important evidence-based advice to the legislature and the public. To assure objectivity, it is insular, being the only organ able to appoint and impeach its own members.

Composition

The Council of Philosophers and Scientists would be composed of twenty-one members serving terms limited by the shorter of seven years, the member resigning, dying or becoming otherwise incapacitated, or by impeachment and trial. The initial council would be nominated by the Secretary General and confirmed by the General Assembly. Thereafter, when a vacancy occurs, the council would nominate and confirm its own members, according to its own rules. To be eligible for the Council of Philosophers and Scientists, a person would be recognized by peers as a leader in a field of science, philosophy, or economics, have integrity, and professional and moral rigor. Unless waived by a two-thirds majority of the existing council, no member could have served elected public office.

Functions

The council's primary function would be to study and declare the social utility of any action of the United Nations. The term "social utility" as used in the Model, means the measure of good an action will confer to all the people of the world. The council also has oversight, appointive, and substitutionary functions throughout the Model.

Checks and Balances

The council could impeach a member for high crimes and abuse of office, or for conduct deemed disqualifying, by majority vote of the non-accused members. Once impeached, the member can be removed from office on trial and conviction by the International Court of Justice, presided by the Chief Judge.

World Central Reserve Bank

The World Central Reserve Bank is an innovation under the Model, providing global monetary policy, and one global currency. The bank's important innovations to central banking are public ownership, and real transparency.

Composition

The World Central Reserve Bank would consist of a board of seven governors serving terms limited by the shorter of seven years, the governor resigning, dying or becoming otherwise incapacitated, or by impeachment and trial. Board members would be nominated by the Economic and Social Council and confirmed by the General Assembly. The initial board of governors would draft a charter, and present it to the General Assembly for approval. Thereon, the bank's charter could be amended only by the positive vote of five governors, and ratified by majority vote of the General Assembly. Once ratified by the General Assembly, the charter of the World Central Reserve Bank would be binding on all Members

Functions

The bank's purpose would be to maximize the social utility of monetary policy, and increase or decrease the money supply, in order to maintain economic stability, giving due consideration to its

Global Governance

primary obligations to promote global economic justice, and to control global economic inequality.

Checks and Balances

The Members shall be the bank's sole shareholders. They would be offered shares in proportion of their gross domestic product to the world gross domestic product. Should any Member decline to purchase shares, their unpurchased share would be offered to the other Members, proportionally. The bank's records would be publicly available. The board of governors would conduct an independent third-party audit of the bank every seven years, which would also be publicly available.

MANAGING CURRENT AND EMERGING CHALLENGES AND RISKS

The Model adds several innovations designed to address structural problems common among most modern governance models, as well as innovations geared to both current and emerging risks and challenges, including the greatest existing threat to world order – unchecked multinational corporate economic power.

Reasonable Controls on Capital

The accumulation of wealth by the shareholders and managers of multinational corporations made possible by global free trade, presents an existential threat to the nation-state. Economic power is ascendant and, because a capitalist's only motivation is profit, by definition, the public good is not served while this dynamic continues.

There is a power shift underway, from the world's governments, to multinational corporations. For instance, under the Trans-Pacific

Global Governance

Partnership, governments (read: taxpayers) are required to pay damages to "investors" (read: capitalists) if the government's laws are enforced in an "arbitrary or unjustifiable manner" or if they "materially impair" the investor's TPP property rights.[2] This isn't just corporate welfare, it's a voluntary cessation of sovereignty. Further, TPP and similar trade agreements shift judicial power from national courts to private arbitration panels. Shifting power from nation-states to multinationals benefits only the multinationals and their shareholders, at the expense of all others. This power shift must be checked, or the nation-state itself could be threatened.

A governance model could theoretically dispense with the nation-state in favor of some new arrangement of power. That would be unwise, as multinational economic power would quickly fill the void, resulting in a corporatoc-

---

[2] Trans Pacific Partnership, Secs. 9.10.3(h), 9.14.1

racy. This Model seeks to strengthen the nation-state, and bring the very productive power of capital under its control, so that economic and political power can be in balance. The Model features four commonly known checks on capital: the cadaster, a progressive tax on capital, a progressive tax on income, and limits on intellectual property rights. It adds one innovation: an annual determination of the state of global economic justice, embodied in what is called the "economic justice factor."

Cadaster

To control capital, one must first know where it is. Picketty said, "[I]f democracy is to regain control over the globalized financial capitalism of this century, it must also invent new tools, adapted to today's challenges." (Picketty, 2014) His solution begins with a cadastral survey, where "[e]veryone would be required to report ownership of capital assets to the world's financial authorities in order to be recognized as the legal owner, with all the advantages and disadvantages thereof." The benefit of the cadaster is that it would "expose wealth to democratic scrutiny, which is a necessary condition for effective regulation of the banking system and international capital flows."

The primary purpose of the cadaster is to collect reliable data, which economists agree is a significant weakness at present. Another purpose is to eliminate the ownerless assets and stateless "non dom" corporations that are all-too-comment creatures of creative legal tax avoidance.

Under the Model, to be recognized as the legal owner of any property, the owner must annually report its existence and estimated value. The Economic and Social Council has jurisdiction to compel Members, legal entities, financial institutions and other custodians of wealth, and persons to make this report, and will use the data to compile a cadaster of the world's wealth. While the task may seem daunting, in the computer age, it is certainly achievable. It might also change the way that people think about property.

Progressive Tax on Capital

Picketty is not the only economist advocating a progressive tax on capital as a check on economic inequality brought on in the age of global capital. The growing social democratic movement in the United States is built on the taxation of extreme wealth, in order to benefit society as a whole. Picketty makes the point: "The ideal tool would be a progressive global tax on capital, coupled with a very high level of international financial transparency." He makes the point several times, repeating the phrase "endless inegalitarian spiral" several times to describe the current problem. As he puts it, "The primary purpose of the capital tax [would not be] to finance the social state, but to regulate capitalism. The goal is first to stop the indefinite increase of inequality of wealth, and second to impose effective regulation on the financial and banking system in order to avoid crises."

The Model gives the General Assembly a mandate to pass a progressive tax on capital, but gives no further guidance other than stating that its purpose is to "keep economic inequality within the limits of the global economic justice factor." The global economic justice factor will be discussed in more detail, below.

Progressive Tax on Income

Picketty distinguishes between wealth and income, finding that there are gross inequalities in both, concluding that his findings "indicate that levying confiscatory rates on top incomes is not only possible but also the only way to stem the observed increase in very high salaries."

The Model authorizes the General Assembly to enact a progressive income tax, and exempts persons making less than the United Nations average income, or less than their national average income. The Model has a similar exemption for capital taxes.

Limits on Intellectual Property Rights

There is widespread recognition of the need for a global system of intellectual property rights. The Model allows for such a system, but provides that "no

Global Governance

such right shall extend beyond twenty years for copyright, and five years for patents." This is a rather crude device, but new national laws and international treaties tend to extend these rights, with negative social utility.

Global Economic Justice Factor

The capitalist's only motive is profit, it is built into our current economic system. The problem, as highlighted by Picketty, is that society in general does not necessarily benefit from a pure capital model. The social/capital system proposed in the Model allows both the capitalist and society to benefit. Controlling capital does not mean taking it all away. It means achieving a balance where innovation, risk, and hard work are rewarded, and society benefits from this effort, as it should, since the reward, profit, comes from society.

Patrick Goggins

Once the cadaster has been performed, the Model mandates that the General Assembly, with the advice of the Council of Philosophers and Scientists, put that data to use, to determine a global economic justice factor, which is a dual determination of the existing levels of economic inequality, and the desirable levels of economic inequality. It can be done globally or regionally. The purpose of the economic justice factor is to maximize the social utility of global capital, recognizing that high levels of economic inequality are unjust and destabilizing, and that total economic equality is neither achievable nor desirable.

Perhaps this environment will make capitalists think differently. Under the Model's social utility ethic, innovation, risk, and hard work are rewarded when they benefit society, as opposed to the current securitization ethic, which seeks only to extract value in the endless search for profit.

Limits on Corporate Participation in Elections

Article 96 of the Model provides that campaign donations and political speech by corporations and other legal entities can be regulated by law. The Model avoids wholescale denial of corporate participation in politics, as those limitations can be used anti-democratically, such as to suppress the press.

Social Utility Index

The focus on social utility is at the heart of the Model's functionality. Under the Model, the Council of Philosophers and Scientists could assign a social utility rating to any action of the United Nations. Social utility is a grounded in the utilitarianism of Jeremy Bentham and John Stewart Mill. In the Model, it is defined as "the measure of good or harm an action will confer to all the people of the world."

The conversation about public affairs can become myopic. Big ideas are what keeps a society healthy, but too often big ideas get lost in minutiae, or are branded as impossible to achieve, in order to make them impossible to achieve. Established power interests are rarely served when there are big changes. Small, incremental changes allow them to adjust and maintain power.

The Model's focus on social utility may not necessarily change this dynamic, but it will force everyone in the discussion to be aware of the big picture, the greater benefit. What's more, if the Council of Philosophers and Scientists assigns a negative social utility rating to a bill, its opponents would have a strong argument against it.

The Big Three

Capitalists have increased profits by moving jobs to places with minimal protections for workers and the environment, which are unfailingly more profitable. As currently practiced, this practice yields negative social utility. Under the Model, the General Assembly would have the power to regulate commerce, labor, and the environment. The intent of this feature is for the General Assembly to set base levels of worker and environmental protections, while also encouraging sustainable growth in developing countries, in order to level the playing field, and maximize commercial social utility.

Genocide and Ethnic Cleansing

Genocide and ethnic cleansing are specifically referred to as human rights abuses justifying the invocation of Chapter VII military powers, and sovereign powers to protect refugees.

Military Spending

The United States is in the process of passing a $760 billion military budget, as much as the next ten nations combined. This is not just bad economic policy, it is also a source of international instability. Far from the fabled *pax Americana*, in the years since World War II, the U.S. military and intelligence regime has been an agent of corporate colonialism, changing foreign regimes to suit America's profit driven adventures.

The Model eliminates the permanent seat status for the P-5, along with their so-called veto power. So, in the unlikely event that the United States remains a Member of a post-Model United Nations, its military would be subject to the Security Council's regulatory jurisdiction, in terms of the amount and types of armaments it manufactures.

The Model also contains a ban on biological, chemical, and nuclear weapons, and similar weapons of mass destruction.

Global Governance

These features are intended to realize the international peace aspired to in the 1945 Charter, and incrementally advanced in subsequent treaties. While having some weapons is probably necessary, and having too many weapons itself become a source of conflict, having a balance of weapons is an effective way to assure world peace.

Intelligence Agencies

The Model provides that any intelligence agency of the United Nations must operate subject to the joint authority of the Security Council and the Secretary-General. Any intelligence agency's meetings would be open to the public, and its records shall be published electronically, unless otherwise provided by law. No law could hinder the right of the Security Council and the Secretary-General to attend any meeting of any intelligence agency, to obtain copies of any record of any intelligence agency, or to disclose any portion of said records or meetings to the General Assembly.

International Military and Economic Agreements

Under the Model, regional military and economic agreements would be subject to the United Nations' authority. Military agreements, for instance, must conform with the Security Council's system for regulation of armaments. Likewise, regional economic agreements are subject to review and approval by the Economic and Social Council, and parties aggrieved under these agreements have a non-waivable right to seek relief before the International Court of Justice.

Travel and Naturalization

Under the Model, the General Assembly would have authority to regulate international travel, including the power to issue one global passport. Further, it contemplates a uniform system of naturalization among the United Nations. This does not mean opening borders, it means having one platform to control population movement. In the event of war, genocide, or ethnic cleansing, the United Nations' power over population movement would become sovereign.

Home Rule/Indigenous Persons

Chapter XI of the 1945 Charter entitled "Declaration Regarding Non-Self-Governing Territories" is renamed in the Model "Declaration Regarding Colonies and Indigenous Persons." The 1945 Charter pre-dated the colonial wars, where occupied territories sought home rule. As a result, its statement on colonies was at best, tepid.

There are currently sixteen colonies in the world, most are held by the U.S. and England. Under the Model, Members holding colonies must present and implement a plan to achieve home rule for the colonies within five years, after which time, if not achieved, the General Assembly may by special law place the colony under its sovereign jurisdiction, to complete the home rule process. In the meantime, the Member is prohibited from extracting any economic benefit from the colony, except that which is necessary to establish home rule.

Further, the Model contains a process where if the people of a geographically contiguous portion of a Member, or Members, desire to separate sovereign bonds with a Member, or Members, and establish sovereign home rule, their duly appointed representatives may petition the Secretary-General, who may convene a joint session of the Security Council, Economic and Social Council, and Council of Philosophers and Scientists to consider the petition. The Secretary-General would chair the proceedings. The joint session would consider evidence given by all interested and affected parties, as well as have the authority to commission its own studies of the petition. The joint session would then make written recommendations, which the Secretary-General would transmit to the General Assembly, which would be adopted on majority vote of both houses.

The model also recognizes that indigenous peoples, culturally distinct people who predate the Member's existence, have the right to be free from cultural hegemony, the right to occupied lands, and the right to levels of self-determination that are consistent with free people.

Political Parties

George Washington warned that political parties "agitate[] the Community with ill-founded jealousies and false alarms." John Adams called them "the greatest political evil under our Constitution." Still, political parties found their way into U.S. government, as with most modern national governments.

Political parties provide only intellectual laziness, legitimized public corruption, and tribal dissent, all of which serve the powerful, not the people.

The Model does not ban political parties, as that would be an affront to free speech and freedom of association, but it does ban them from the United Nations. It provides that "No law or rule of the United Nations shall empower, give procedural recognition, or otherwise give preference to political parties or similar factions. The United Nations shall not recognize political parties, except as entities to be taxed."

Term Limits

It has been said that an officeholder has seven years' worth of political capital. After that, a person seeks only to remain in power, and the means this is accomplished is often corrupt. Term limits solve this problem though, admittedly, they can create new problems.

Every office in the Model is term limited, except for judges in the International Court of Justice, and its lower courts.

The problem with term limits is they tend to shift power to the professional bureaucracy. To counter (but not necessarily solve) this problem, the Model requires: a) a joint session of the General Assembly for any bill that would create a new agency, and b) that the Secretary-General annually propose a list of laws to be repealed. The Council of Philosophers and Scientists must assign a social utility rating to each repeal.

Public Records and Meetings

Supreme Court Justice Louis Brandeis once said that sunshine is the best disinfectant. While most public records and meetings laws are statutory, the Model includes it in the Charter, to express the importance of integrity in government.

Public records must be electronic form under the Model, with one print copy kept by the archivist. The Model's public meetings provision is modeled on Florida's relatively successful Sunshine in Government Act.

Single Subject Limitation

In the United States, almost every state has a single subject limitation in its constitution. A single subject limitation is exactly what it says it is: a constitutional limitation that each bill can address only one subject. It seems uncontroversial, until one considers that the U.S. Constitution does not have one. The result has been "pork barrel" bills that combine completely unrelated provisions, usually to subvert the usual legislative process. The result is diminished confidence in the process.

Global Governance

The Model contains a single subject limitation, which acts as an important procedural check on the General Assembly's legislative powers. It also provides that spending bills can only address spending, and a requirement that the bill voted on by both houses be identical, eliminating the anti-democratic practice of re-drafting legislation after the vote, in conference.

Standard Pitch

Although not a conventional constitutional issue, the Model contains a provision that the standard concert pitch be set at A = 431.4757 hz. The current standard, 440 hz (ISO-16:1975), is controversial, was adopted under suspicious circumstances, and although not thoroughly tested, there is anecdotal evidence that this pitch is harmful to people. There is anecdotal evidence that 431.4757 hz is more pleasing than the current standard, and is actually quite healthful.

Patrick Goggins

III. ARGUMENT

To be successful, a system of governance must balance both political and economic power.

The Model is an all-of-the-above collection of good governance ideas, and features good economic theory to good political theory. In practice, money and power are the same thing. The Model's central premise is that balancing political power means nothing if economic power isn't also controlled in some manner.

Under the Model, economic power is controlled by an evidence-based, rational balance between the interests of capitalists and society. This system assures high performance and its own longevity, because both political and economic power are allowed the proper space. The Model encourages innovation and efficiency, while maintaining a thoughtful level of economic justice. Risk and hard work are rewarded, but not at the expense of society as a whole.

Core Values

There are two main ways that the Model advances the common good. First, by subjecting every action taken by the United Nations to a social utility analysis. Second, by giving the United Nations definite core values.

Social Utility

The Model's innovation with respect to core values is its emphasis on social utility. Under the Model, every action of the United Nations is subject to scrutiny for social utility. By definition, social utility measures each human as being equal. Before the General Assembly votes on a bill, it is given a social utility rating by the Council of Philosophers and Scientists. That way, the world will know whether, according to our best minds, the law would be in everyone's best interest.

Definite Values

The Model maintains the core values of the 1945 Charter, but makes them more definite. The values expressed in the 1945 Charter are, by necessity, indefinite. For instance, the Article 1 principles are *to take effective collective measures* for the prevention and removal of threats to the peace, to *develop* friendly relations among nations, and to *achieve international co-operation* in solving international problems. The Model's core values are definite. Its Article 1 principles are to *prevent and remove* threats to peace, to *secure* friendly relations among nations, and to *solve* international problems. While these changes only go to tone, they convey an important message about the United Nation's strengthened mission under the Model.

Decision-Making Capacity

The process of enacting laws is necessarily deliberative. The impacts of new laws must be carefully studied, and due process requires that all potentially affected people be informed, and given the right to be heard. This takes time, and it should take time.

Once well-placed legislation is enacted, timing and adequacy is a function of execution. Under the Model, executive jurisdiction primarily falls under the Secretary-General, although the Security Council, the Economic and Social, the Council of Philosophers and Scientists, and the World Central Reserve Bank, all have discrete executive functions, which are carefully defined under the Model. The Model also provides for cooperation between the organs, for instance, by allowing the International Court of Justice to issue advisory opinions, a feature that exists under the 1945 Charter.

Finally, by maintaining and improving the existing structure of the United Nations, the Model is ready for real world transition. It does not seek to re-invent the wheel, it merely puts the wheels under a much stronger engine.

Effectiveness

Jurisdiction is the essence of government. Put another way, a government must have jurisdiction, or it is not a government. Obviously, without jurisdiction, an organization like the United Nations is "global governance without global government." Only jurisdiction can give the organization the power to effect change for the common good. Some may argue that stitching together loose webs of like-minded groups in a mutually cooperative polycentric networks would just as effectively meet our needs in the day of international commerce, but faced with the economic power of global capital, that network would be like a kite in a hurricane. The jurisdiction provided under the Model makes the United Nations strong as a jet airplane and, wisely guided, would much more likely secure the common good.

What is important is that the jurisdiction granted under the Model is limited. The Member nation-state, and its subsidiary organs, are and should be the primary source of day-to-day *intra-national* government. What occurs under the Model is, generally, *international* government. So just as the American states retain a level of sovereignty under the United States, the Member nations states would retain a level of sovereignty under the United Nations. This layer of international governance would cause minimal disruption to the world's existing governmental structures. The main difference would be that, under the Model, the differences between nation-states would be resolved in the best interests of all people, not just the powerful.

Resources and Financing

The Model provides for sufficient human and material resources to accomplish its mission, which includes achieving economic justice for all people.

Human Resources

The Model provides for staffing of the United Nations, with express appointment and election criteria for Charter-level positions, and authorized staff-level hiring. The paramount consideration in the employment of the staff and in the determination of the conditions of service under the Model is the necessity of securing the highest standards of efficiency, competence, and integrity. Due regard would be paid to the importance of recruiting the staff on as wide a geographical basis as possible, with proportional representation in the staff by gender, race, religion, sexual preference, sexual expression, age, ethnic origin, or national origin.

Material Resources

The Model provides for progressive taxation of income and capital to fund itself. Taxes have the dual purpose of funding the United Nations, and promoting economic justice. Taxes are determined on income and asset determinations made by the Economic and Social Council. That data is paired with the economic justice factor, which is determined by the General Assembly, with the advice of the Council of Philosophers and Scientists.

As Thomas Jefferson said: "The property of this country is absolutely concentred in a very few hands ... I am conscious that an equal division of property is impracticable, but the consequences of this enormous inequality producing so much misery to the bulk of mankind, legislators cannot invent too many devices for subdividing property, only taking care to let their subdivisions go hand in hand with the natural affections of the human mind." Letter to James Madison, October 28, 1785.

The purpose of the economic justice factor is to maximize the social utility of the taxing and redistribution of economic assets, recognizing that high levels of economic inequality are unjust and destabilizing, and that total economic equality is neither achievable nor desirable.

The economic justice factor is then used to determine the level of taxes on income and capital.

There are protections for the poor built into the Model. It prohibits income taxes on any person making less than the United Nations average income, or less than their national average income, and capital taxes on any person having a net worth less than the United Nations average net worth, or less than their national average net worth. Other worthy methods of achieving economic justice, such as a basic income, a social dividend, or a minimum inheritance, are left out of the Model, but could be enacted by legislation.

Trust and Insight

Like all human relations, trust in government is initially assumed, is easily lost, and once lost, is difficult to regain. The Model maximizes structural protections that, properly executed, would minimize the incidence of lost trust. It also has corrective measures which allow it to regain trust, once lost.

Trust

It is no accident that the word "integrity" occurs five times in the Model. Good government begins with the selection of good people, but it doesn't end there. Ronald Reagan popularized the phrase "trust but verify." The primary verification mechanisms built into the Model are the public records and public meetings provisions, discussed above. These provisions are quite common as laws, but they are raised to Charter-level priorities in the Model. No resolution, rule, or formal action shall be considered binding except as taken or made at a properly noticed public meeting.

Insight

The Model's very structure is intended to balance power, both political and economic. The

Global Governance

Model is founded on the ancient and reliable tri-partite separation of political powers, between the legislative, executive, and judicial. Its major innovation is the ability to control economic power, effectively absent in world governance today. The Model controls economic power, promoting economic justice by progressive taxation, enlightened by the in-depth social utility analysis, discussed above.

Political power is controlled by checks and balances. Appointments and actions are the two points where checks and balances are most effective. Both points are affected by the Model's limitation of the corrupting influence of economic power. This is accomplished generally by progressive taxation and the economic justice factor, and specifically by limitations on corporate involvement in elections, and political speech.

Also vital to the Model's effectiveness are the protections against the abuse of power, discussed below.

Patrick Goggins

Appointments

The power to appoint is the power to control. Under the Model, the members of each organ are appointed by members of other organs, or in the case of the People's Assembly, elected outright. The sole exception is the Council of Philosophers and Scientists, which after the initial composition, appoints its own members. This is to encourage an insular, fact-driven enterprise, free from outside influences.

Term limits are another facet of appointments, which ensure the health of the system under the Model. Human nature being what it is, it is understandable that, once in power, one would want to remain in power. In the Model, this often corrupting desire is eliminated by term limits. The International Court of Justice is the sole exception. Lifetime judicial terms distance judges from their appointive nominators, allowing experience and good judgment to carry the day.

Actions

Under the Model, once an organ is constituted, its actions are subject to revision and, in some cases, veto by other organs. The International Court of Justice can also nullify any action that exceeds the United Nations' jurisdiction. In addition, every action of the United Nations can be assigned a social utility rating by the Council of Philosophers and Scientists, exposing the benefits or harm of what was accomplished.

Flexibility

Amending the Charter is difficult by design, but the high threshold can discourage worthy ideas, because of the effort involved. With the exception of eliminating the P-5, the amendment process set forth in Chapter XVIII of the 1945 charter remains unchanged under the Model: two-thirds of the General Assembly, and two-thirds of Members are required before an amendment is ratified.

The Model adds a general conference, every seven years, for review of the Charter. This encourages needed structural changes in the Model. In anticipation of the conference, the Secretary-General, the Security Council, the Economic and Social Council, and the Council of Philosophers and Scientists must submit recommended Charter amendments for consideration by the general conference, to which the which the Council of Philosophers and Scientists will assign social utility ratings, which then will pass upon two-thirds vote of the Members in the general conference, and ratified by two-thirds of the Members.

Protection against the Abuse of Power

There are three primary mechanisms built in to the Model to protect against the abuse of power: the courts, the code of ethics, and the social utility ratings. Initially though, it is important to note that favoring one group over another is not necessarily an abuse of power. When public institutions act, there are always winners and losers. The important question is whether, in terms of social utility, they were the right winners and losers.

First is the limited nature of the United Nations' jurisdiction. In the normal course, if a law or an executive action oversteps the United Nation's limited jurisdiction in the Model, a jurisdictional challenge to that law or executive action can be taken to the International Court of Justice, which can nullify any action of any other organ.

Second are the provisions against public corruption. The Model calls for a code of ethics, which includes in the definition of abuse of office "exchanging official actions for personal gain, directly or indirectly, including gain for a family member." Under the Model, a Charter-level appointee *can* be impeached for abuse of office, and a staff member *must* be fired for abuse of office. The Model goes so far as to provide for criminal sanctions, and claw-back provisions for ill-gotten gains.

Third is the assignment of social utility ratings by the Council of Philosophers and Scientists. Although these ratings have no jurisdictional component in the Model, they are intended to publicize the helpful and harmful actions of the United Nations' organs. Combined with the public meetings and public records provisions, the exposure would tend to discourage abuse of power.

Accountability

Under the Model, individual decision-makers are held accountable for abuse of office, but the system is ultimately responsible for its own performance. The Model provides the United Nations with sufficient authority to accomplish its mission, with sufficient structural safeguards to provide for effective government.

Performance

The Model gives the United Nations limited jurisdiction, which would necessarily give it the power to perform its appointed tasks. The decision-makers are either Charter-level or staff-level actors who are limited to only the actions allowed under the Model's jurisdictional schema. If their actions exceed the jurisdictional grant, they can be challenged before the International Court of Justice, which can nullify actions which exceed the United Nations' jurisdiction.

Accountability

Most Charter-level decision-makers are term limited under the Model, which is a structural limit on their power. The sole exception are the judges on the International Court of Justice, who have life terms. This serves the important interest of maintaining an independent judiciary. Charter-level actors can be impeached for high crimes and abuse of office, while staff must be fired for abuse of office. Again, abuse of office is defined in the Model as "exchanging official actions for personal gain, directly or indirectly, including gain for a family member."

Finally, under the Model, the World Central Reserve Bank's records and meetings are public, and it is required to undergo an outside audit every three years.

IV. CONCLUSION

A recent New York Times editorial lamented that, "For all its resilience and longevity, our Constitution doesn't have structural checks built into it to prevent oligarchy or populist demagogues."[3] What's true for the United States' Constitution is true many times over for the 1945 United Nations Charter. We are at a critical time where nuclear weapons, climate change, and historic levels of economic inequality are well known, and the democratic mechanisms of the nation-state are still sufficiently strong to correct the looming crises.

And the crises are looming. Nuclear war can begin on Twitter. Climate change is already happening. As for economic inequality, capitalism's only motivation is profit. If capital is not controlled, rising economic power will weaken the political power of democratic nation-states, and economic inequality will reach

---

[3] Ganesh Sitaraman, "Our Constitution Wasn't Built for This" (New York Times, September 16, 2017).

proportions where whole populations will be left with no choice but general insurrection. People will do what they must to survive. If the "endless inegalitarian spiral" continues, and the people's voices are not heard, they will have no choice but to resort to arms. The oligarchy's military response could be devastating.

But there is still time. The Model is certainly just one of many new ideas about global governance. The discussion of global governance, and global government, has been a possibility since the Peace of Westphalia. And while globalization has had many negative effects, it has also made us more familiar with one another, and as a result, likely more amendable to entering into a binding power-sharing arrangement, such as the one proposed in the Model.

The next action must be to continue talking about global government, but that cannot be the last action. An important milestone would be to have the United Nations consider amending its Charter to add any sort of jurisdiction.

Global Governance

Most important, though, is to realize that the cost of inaction could be immeasurably high.

Patrick Goggins

APPENDIX I

UN Charter (amended)

WE THE PEOPLES OF THE UNITED NATIONS, DETERMINED

- to save succeeding generations from the scourge of war, which throughout history, has brought untold sorrow to mankind, and

- to secure and protect fundamental human rights, the dignity and worth of the person, and the equal rights of men and women and of nations large and small, and

- to secure and maintain international social and economic justice, and the social and economic advancement of all peoples; and

- to respect the obligations arising from treaties and other sources of international law, and

- to promote social progress and better standards of life in larger freedom,

AND FOR THESE ENDS, DETERMINED

- to provide an integrated system of international governance, with limited jurisdiction; and

- to practice tolerance and live together in peace with one another as good neighbours, and

- to unite our strength to maintain international peace and security, and

- to ensure that armed force shall not be used, save in the common interest

- to employ international machinery for the promotion of the economic and social advancement of all peoples

HAVE RESOLVED TO COMBINE OUR EFFORTS TO ACCOMPLISH THESE AIMS

Accordingly, our respective Governments, through representatives assembled in the city of _____, who are all duly authorized to enter into this Amended Charter, which has found to be in good and due form, have agreed to this Amended Charter of the United Nations, which amends and restates the charter previously adopted on 26 June 1945 in San Francisco.

CHAPTER I: PURPOSES AND PRINCIPLES

Article 1 - Purposes

The United Nations' power is derived from the people, and belongs to the people.[4] The Purposes of the United Nations are:

1. To maintain international peace and security, and to that end: to prevent and remove threats to peace, to suppress acts of aggression or other breaches of the peace, to prevent human rights abuses such as genocide or ethnic cleansing, and to adjust or settle international disputes or situations which might lead to a breach of the peace, by peaceful means, and in conformity with the principles of social utility, justice and international law;

2. To maximize social utility of public and private processes and institutions, social and economic

---

[4] C.a. Chinese 1982 constitution, Art. 2

justice among all people, and to control capital towards those ends;

3. To secure friendly relations among nations, based on respect for the principle of equal rights and self-determination of peoples, and to take other appropriate measures to strengthen universal peace;

4. To solve international problems of an economic, social, cultural, or humanitarian character, and in promoting and encouraging respect for human rights and for fundamental freedoms for all without distinction as to gender, race, religion, sexual preference, sexual expression, age, ethnic origin, or national origin;

5. To promote home rule and self-governance among all people; and

6. To enact and enforce laws in the attainment of these common ends, within its limited jurisdiction.

7. Social utility as that term is used in this Charter, means the measure of good or harm an action will confer to all the people of the world. In the analysis, all persons shall be deemed equal.

Global Governance

Article 2 - Principles

The United Nations and its Members, in pursuit of the Purposes stated in Article 1, shall act in accordance with the following Principles.

1. The United Nations is based on the principle of the sovereign equality of all its Members.

2. All Members, in order to ensure to all of them the rights and benefits resulting from membership, shall comply with laws enacted in accordance with the present Charter. Any nation failing to comply with laws enacted in accordance with the present Charter is subject to suspension and expulsion

3. All Members shall settle their international disputes by peaceful means in such a manner that international peace and security, and justice, are not endangered.

4. All Members shall refrain in their international relations from the threat or use of force against the territorial integrity or political independence of any state, or in any other manner inconsistent with the Purposes of the United Nations. Any nation threatening or using force against any state in violation of this Charter is subject to suspension and expulsion.

5. No Member will conduct, or allow its citizens to conduct, economic activity of any kind with states or the citizens of states which are not Members of the United Nations. The sole exception is personal use expenses for travel by Member citizens to non-Member countries, or by non-Member citizens to Member countries.

6. Nothing contained in the present Charter shall authorize the United Nations to intervene in matters which are essentially within the domestic jurisdiction of any state or shall require the Members to submit such matters to settlement under the present Charter; but this principle shall not prejudice the application of enforcement measures under Chapter VII.

7. No law or rule of the United Nations shall empower, give procedural recognition, or otherwise give preference to political parties or similar factions. The United Nations shall not recognize political parties, except as entities to be taxed.

CHAPTER II: MEMBERSHIP

Article 3 – Initial Composition and Transition

1. The Members of the United Nations shall be the states which, having participated in the United Nations Conference on International Organization at _____, have ratified this amended Charter.

2. Upon ratification of the Amendment, financial and personal property owned by non-Member citizens in Member countries will be returned to the non-Member citizens. Real property owned by non-Member citizens in Member countries will be sold to member citizens, and the proceeds returned to the non-Member citizen. Thereafter, property owned by non-Member citizens will be treated as set forth in Article 4 and Article 5.

3. Each existing organ of the United Nations shall immediately implement those changes to its structure and rules necessary to implement the Amendment. Members shall conform their laws to this Charter. The first elections shall take place on _____, 20__.

Article 4 – Admission of New Members

4. Membership in the United Nations is open to all other peace-loving states which accept and agree, on behalf of themselves and all persons and legal entities under their jurisdiction, to be bound by the obligations contained in the present Charter, as amended, and, in the judgment of the United Nations, are able and willing to carry out these obligations.

5. The admission of any such state to membership in the United Nations will be effected by a decision of the General Assembly upon petition by duly appointed representatives of the state to the Secretary-General, who may convene a joint session of the Security Council, Economic and Social Council, and Council of Philosophers and Scientists to consider the petition. The Secretary-General shall chair the proceedings. The joint session shall consider evidence given by all interested and affected parties, as well as have the authority to commission its own studies of the petition. The joint session shall make written recommendations, which the Secretary-General shall transmit to the General Assembly, which shall be adopted on majority vote of both houses.

6. Should the people of a geographically contiguous portion of a Member, or Members, desire to separate juridical bonds with a Member, or Members, and establish sovereign home rule, their duly appointed representatives may petition the Secretary-General, who may convene a joint session of the Security Council, Economic and Social Council, and Council of Philosophers and Scientists to consider the petition. The Secretary-General shall chair the proceedings. The joint session shall consider evidence given by all interested and affected parties, as well as have the authority to commission its own studies of the petition. The joint session shall make written recommendations, which the Secretary-General shall transmit to the General Assembly, which shall be adopted on majority vote of both houses.

Article 5 – Suspension

A Member of the United Nations against which preventive or enforcement action has been taken by the Secretary-General, the Security Council, the Economic and Social Council, or the International Court of Justice, may be suspended by the General Assembly upon majority vote of both houses. A Member may also be suspended by order of the International Court of Justice pursuant to Article ___. Member states are authorized, within their respective jurisdictions, to seize the property of suspended

Members, and their citizens, and hold the same until the suspension is lifted, in which case it shall be returned to the suspended Member and its citizens. The General Assembly may also impose such other sanctions or conditions on relief of suspension as it deems fit. Members and their citizens may conduct economic activity with suspended Members, subject to limitations imposed by the General Assembly.

Article 6 – Expulsion

A suspended Member of the United Nations which has failed to cure the cause of suspension may be expelled from the United Nations by the General Assembly upon a majority vote of bother houses, and ratified by the Secretary-General. No Member will conduct, or allow its citizens to conduct, economic activity of any kind with states, or the citizens of states, which are expelled Members of the United Nations. On expulsion, any property held by Member states of the expelled Member or its citizens shall be handed over to the United Nations and may be used for such purposes as the United Nations sees fit. No portion of this property shall be returned to the expelled member or its citizens unless and until the expelled Member state has be re-admitted. An expelled Member may only be re-admitted upon cure of the cause for expulsion, and re-admission pursuant to Article 4.

CHAPTER III: ORGANS

Article 7 – Seven Organs

1. There are established seven principal organs of the United Nations: a General Assembly, a Security Council, an Economic and Social Council, an International Court of Justice, a Secretariat, a Council of Philosophers and Scientists, and a World Central Reserve Bank.

2. The power of the organs are limited to those set forth in this Charter. All other powers are retained by the Members, or the people.

3. Such subsidiary organs as may be found necessary may be established in accordance with the present Charter.

4. Any Member that is suspended or expulsed from the United Nations pursuant to this Charter shall automatically lose its seat on the organs and subsidiary organs of the United Nations.

Article 8 – Hiring, Records, and Meetings

1. The United Nations shall not discriminate or place requirements or restrictions which have a discriminatory effect, on the basis of gender,

race, religion, sexual preference, sexual expression, age, ethnic origin, or national origin.

2. There is established the United Nations Archives[5], under the Secretary-General, which shall be the custodian for all records of the United Nations, which consists of documents created by, on behalf of, or submitted to any agency, board, or commission of the United Nations. The records of the United Nations shall be in electronic form, unless print copies are necessary. The archivist shall create one paper copy of each public record. Unless exempted by law, the records the United Nations are open for personal inspection and copying by any person. Providing access to public records is a duty of each agency, board, and commission of the United Nations.

3. All meetings of any agency, board, or commission of the United Nations, shall public meetings open to the public at all times, except as otherwise provided by law. This includes regularly scheduled meetings, as well as meetings by any person with, or attended by, any person elected to such agency, board, or commission, whether or not that person has yet taken office, at which

---

[5] Successor of the Archives and Records Management Section.

Global Governance

official actions are to be taken. No resolution, rule, or formal action shall be considered binding except as taken or made at such meeting. The agency, board, or commission must provide reasonable notice of all such meetings, and transcripts or recordings of said meetings shall be published electronically, and made permanently available to the public. The records of said meetings shall include the yeas and nays of the members on any question.

4. The International Court of Justice shall have jurisdiction to issue injunctions to enforce Section 7(3) and Section 7(4). The Secretary-General shall determine whether a record or meeting can be exempt from this requirement, in accordance with procedures established by the General Assembly, but even if exempt, records, transcripts or recordings of meetings shall be made, and permanently retained by the Secretary-General, until such time as the General Assembly orders them released to the public.

CHAPTER IV: THE GENERAL ASSEMBLY

Article 9 - Composition

Section 9.1 – Elections and Qualifications

1. All legislative Powers herein granted shall be vested in the General Assembly, which shall consist of the Senate and the People's Assembly.

2. Representatives to the People's Assembly shall be elected by popular vote of the people of each Member. Senators shall be appointed by the government of each Member. The Members may not alter the qualifications, term limits, or other restrictions in this Charter. The General Assembly may at any time by law make or alter regulations on appointments or elections. Each house shall be the judge of the appointments, elections, returns and qualifications of its own members.

3. The Senators and Representatives shall receive a salary for their services, to be ascertained by law, and paid out of the treasury of the United Nations.

Global Governance

4. No Senator or Representative shall, during the time for which he or she was elected, be appointed to any other office in the United Nations; and no person holding any office in the United Nations, shall be a member of either house during his or her continuance in office.

5. No Senator or Representative shall be subject to liability or disciplinary action or otherwise be called to account outside of the General Assembly for a vote cast or a statement made in the General Assembly or any of its committees.[6] They shall in all cases, except felony and breach of the peace, be privileged from arrest during their attendance at the session of their respective houses, and in going to and returning from the same; and for any speech or debate in either house, they shall not be questioned in any other place.

Section 9.2 – The People's Assembly

1. The People's Assembly shall be composed of Representatives chosen every seventh year by a simple majority of the people of the Member states, shall be at least twenty-

---

[6] From German constitution Article 46.

one years old, and shall be a citizen of the Member state in which the Representative is chosen. Representatives are limited to one seven-year term in office. If a vacancy occurs, the replacement Representative may only serve out the remaining term, and shall not be eligible for re-election.

2. Representatives shall be apportioned among the Members as follows: each Member shall have its proportionate share of one thousand chairs in the People's Assembly, based on populations of Members, as determined by the most recent census completed by the Economic and Social Council, current as of the date ninety days prior to the election; no Member shall have fewer than one Representative; no Member shall have more than one hundred Representatives.

3. The People's Assembly shall have the sole power of impeachment, except for members of the Council of Philosophers and Scientists.

4. The People's Assembly shall have the sole power of originating appropriations.

Global Governance

Section 9.3 – The Senate

1. The Senate shall be composed of one Senator selected by the government of each Member. Each Senator shall be at least twenty-one years old, and shall be a citizen of the Member state in which the Senator is chosen. Senators' term in office are limited to the shorter of one fourteen-year term, the Senator resigning, dying or becoming otherwise incapacitated, or by impeachment and trial. If a vacancy occurs, the replacement Senator shall commence a new fourteen-year term.

2. The Senate shall have the sole power to try all impeachments. When sitting for that purpose, they shall be on oath or affirmation. And no person shall be convicted without the concurrence of two thirds of the Senators present.

3. Judgment in cases of impeachment shall not extend further than to removal from office, and disqualification to hold and enjoy any other office, trust or profit under the United Nations: but the party convicted shall nevertheless be liable and subject to indictment, trial, judgment and punishment, according to law.

Section 9.4 - Process

1. Bills pertaining to the laying and collection of taxes shall originate with the Economic and Social Council, which shall present the bill to the General Assembly, which may not amend the bill, but may approve the bill by a majority of both houses, and subject to veto by the Secretary-General, which can be overridden by two-thirds majority of both houses of the General Assembly.[7]

2. Each bill shall be presented to the Council of Philosophers and Scientists prior to public hearings on the bill in accordance with Article 86. After being assigned a social utility rating by the Council of Philosophers and Scientists. If the Council of Philosophers and Scientists does not assign a social utility rating within the time set forth in Article 86, the requirement for a social utility rating shall be waived.

3. The presenting house shall have a public hearing prior to a vote by either house, where people may speak in a time and manner determined by the presenting

---

[7] From Elisabeth Jacobs, *Everywhere and Nowhere – Politics in C21*.

Global Governance

house. The public shall also have the opportunity to comment electronically. The public comments shall become part of the record for any legislation.

4. Only bills that have been voted on in identical forms by each house may become law. Any amendment must be presented by a Senator or a Representative in their respective house, whose name shall be assigned to the amendment. A house's review of an amended bill is non-waivable. If an amendment is proposed and passed by one house, the amended bill must be voted and passed by the other house prior to presentment to the Secretary-General.

5. Every bill shall embrace but one subject which shall be expressed in its title, general appropriations laws shall only embrace appropriations, and other appropriations shall be made by separate law, related to the appropriation, embracing but one subject.

6. Every bill which shall have passed the People's Assembly and the Senate in identical form, shall, before it become a law, be presented to the Secretary-General of the United Nations. If the Secretary-General approves he or she shall sign it, but if not,

the Secretary-General shall return it, with objections, to that house in which it originated, who shall proceed to reconsider it. If after such reconsideration two thirds of that house shall agree to pass the bill, it shall be sent, together with the objections, to the other house, by which it shall likewise be reconsidered, and if approved by two thirds of that house, it shall become a law. But in all such cases the votes of both houses shall be determined by yeas and nays, and the names of the persons voting for and against the bill shall be made public record. If any bill shall not be returned by the Secretary-General within ten days after it shall have been presented to him or her, the same shall be a law, in like manner as if he had signed it, unless the General Assembly by their adjournment prevent its return, in which case it shall not be a law.

Article 10 - Powers

The General Assembly shall have power to:

1. Lay and collect taxes, including progressive taxes on income, capital, consumption, pollution, and waste, to pay the debts and provide for the general welfare of the United Nations;

Global Governance

2. To borrow money on the credit of the United Nations; and to issue a single world currency;

3. To regulate commerce among the United Nations, including health and education, and conform international economic and trade agreements to this Charter, and

4. To effect this Charter with respect to non-Members, and Members that have been suspended or expelled;

5. To regulate travel and human migration, including issuing one global passport, and to establish a uniform system of naturalization among the United Nations. These powers become sovereign in the event of genocide, or ethnic cleansing, and to protect civilian refugees of war;

6. To promote the progress of science and useful arts, by securing for limited times to authors and inventors the exclusive right to their respective writings and discoveries, although no such right shall extend beyond twenty years for copyright, and five years for patents;

7. To constitute tribunals inferior to the International Court of Justice, and to admit and regulate specialized agencies;

8. To enact laws regarding emissions, pollution, and waste, protecting the environment and regulating sources of energy;

9. To enact laws protecting workers' rights, workplace safety, and regulating wages and income from labor.

10. To provide for calling forth the militaries of Members to execute the laws of the United Nations; to conform international defense and military agreements to this Charter; to regulated and provide for organizing, arming, and disciplining, the militaries of Members, as they may individually require, and for governing such part of them as may be employed in the service of the United Nations, reserving to the Members respectively, the appointment of the officers, and the authority of training the military according to the discipline prescribed by the General Assembly;

11. To enact laws as sovereign, including criminal laws, over (a) international waters; (b) the extent of earth's domain over outer

Global Governance

space; (c) colonies; (d) Antarctica, and (e) over such district as may, by cession of particular Members, and the acceptance of the General Assembly, become the seat of the government of the United Nations, and to exercise like authority over all places purchased by the consent of the legislature of the Members in which the same shall be, for the erection of such facilities deemed necessary under this Charter; and

12. To make all laws which shall be necessary and proper for carrying into execution the foregoing powers, the rights of persons under the Universal Declaration of Human Rights, and all other powers vested by this Charter in the government of the United Nations, or in any department or officer thereof.

Article 11 - Limitations

1. The privilege of the writ of habeas corpus shall not be suspended.

2. No ex post facto law shall be passed; bills of attainder are allowed only to the extent they apply to non-Members, or Members that have been suspended or expelled.

3. No capitation tax shall be laid, nor shall income tax be levied on any person making less than the United Nations average income, or less than their national average income, nor shall capital tax be levied on any person having a net worth less than the United Nations average net worth, or less than their national average net worth.

4. No tax or duty shall be laid on articles exported from any Member to another Member.

5. No preference shall be given by any regulation of commerce or revenue to the ports of one Member over those of another: nor shall goods or services bound to, or from, one Member, be obliged to enter, clear, or pay duties in another.

6. No money shall be drawn from the treasury, but in consequence of appropriations made by law; and a regular statement and account of the receipts and expenditures of all public money shall be published electronically from time to time.

7. No person holding any office of the United Nations shall, without the consent of the General Assembly, accept of any present,

Global Governance

emolument, office, or title, of any kind whatever, from any king, prince, or foreign state.

8. Every law shall embrace but one subject which shall be expressed in its title, general appropriations laws shall only embrace appropriations, and other appropriations shall be made by separate law, related to the appropriation, embracing but one subject.

9. New laws shall be administered by the existing executive structure. There shall be a joint public session of the General Assembly prior to voting on any bill creating a new administrative agency, where evidence shall be taken on the merits of the need for a new administrative agency.

10. The Secretary-General shall annually recommend to the General Assembly what laws should be repealed. The Council of Philosophers and Scientists shall assign a social utility rating to each proposed repeal, and the General Assembly shall vote on each recommended repeal.

Article 12 – International Peace and Security

1. The Secretary-General, with the consent of the Security Council, shall notify the General Assembly at each session of any matters relative to the maintenance of international peace and security which are being dealt with by the Security Council and shall similarly notify the General Assembly, or the Members of the United Nations if the General Assembly is not in session, immediately if the Security Council ceases to deal with such matters.

2. The General Assembly, upon the affirmative vote of two thirds of each house, an in accordance with Article 42, may order the commencement or cessation of military activity in connection with any matters relative to the maintenance of international peace and security, whether or not they have been reported by the Secretary-General. If any member of the Security Council fails to commence or cease military activity, in derogation of the General Assembly's order, it can be, upon further two thirds vote of each house of the General Assembly, be expelled from the Security Council, and replaced by a Member of the General Assembly's choosing.

Global Governance

Article 13 – Global Economic Justice

1. The General Assembly, with the advice of the Council of Philosophers and Scientists, shall annually set a global economic justice factor, or a set of regional economic justice factors, based on the cadaster provided by the Economic and Social Council pursuant to Article 62. The purpose of the cadaster is to identify and account for significant holdings of global capital, in all its forms. The purpose of the economic justice factor is to maximize the social utility of the distribution of economic assets, recognizing that high levels of economic inequality are unjust and destabilizing, and that total economic equality is neither achievable nor desirable.

2. The General Assembly shall, by law, pass an annual progressive tax on capital. The purpose of such law will be to control capital, in order to keep economic inequality within the limits of the global economic justice factor.

3. The General Assembly may suspend or otherwise sanction any Member which fails to cooperate with or otherwise hinders the cadaster, the annual progressive tax on capital, or otherwise hinders global economic justice.

4. Reporting property to the cadaster is a condition of rights to any property. Any property that is not reported to the cadaster reverts to the United Nations.

Article 14 – General Welfare

Subject to the provisions of Article ___, the General Assembly may by law, pass measures it deems necessary for the peaceful adjustment of any situation, regardless of origin, which it deems likely to impair the general welfare or friendly relations among nations, including situations resulting from a violation of the provisions of the present Charter setting forth the Purposes and Principles of the United Nations, and to **prevent human rights abuses such as genocide or ethnic cleansing**.

Article 15 - Reports

1. The General Assembly shall receive and consider annual and special reports from the Security Council; these reports shall include an account of the measures that the Security Council has decided upon or taken to maintain international peace and security.

2. The General Assembly shall receive and consider reports from the other organs of the United Nations.

Global Governance

Article 16 – Sovereign Jurisdiction

The Members shall maintain sovereign jurisdiction within their borders, except as provided in this Charter. The United Nations has exclusive sovereign jurisdiction over international waters, outer space, and Antarctica. The United Nations also has sovereign jurisdiction over colonies, to the extent that jurisdiction is conferred pursuant to Chapter XI.

Article 17 – Budget and Expenses

1. The General Assembly shall consider and approve the budget of the United Nations, which shall be presented to the Council of Philosophers and Scientists, and rated by them for social utility as set forth in Section 9.4.2 hereto, prior to approval.

2. The expenses of the United Nations shall be borne by taxes, fines, and penalties, as levied by law, by regular income on assets, and by the Members as apportioned by the General Assembly.

3. The General Assembly shall consider and approve any financial and budgetary arrangements with specialized agencies referred to in Article 57 and shall examine the administrative budgets of

such specialized agencies with a view to making recommendations to the agencies concerned.

Article 18 - Voting

1. Each Representative and Senator of the General Assembly shall have one vote.

2. Decisions of the General Assembly on important questions shall be made by a two-thirds majority of the members present and voting. These questions shall include: authorization to use military force, election of the Secretary-General, admission of new Members to the United Nations, suspension of the rights and privileges of membership, expulsion of Members, and amendments to this Charter.

3. Decisions on other questions, including the determination of additional categories of questions to be decided by a two-thirds majority, shall be made by a majority of the members present and voting.

Article 19 – Arrears

A Member of the United Nations which is in arrears in the payment of its financial contributions to the United Nations shall have no vote in the General Assembly if the amount of its arrears equals or exceeds the amount of the contributions due from it for the preceding two full years. The General Assembly may, nevertheless, permit such a Member to vote if it is satisfied that the failure to pay is due to conditions beyond the Member's control.

Article 20 – Procedure

The General Assembly shall meet in regular annual sessions and in such special sessions as occasion may require. Special sessions shall be convoked by the Secretary-General at the request of the Security Council or of a majority of the Members of the United Nations. A majority of each house shall constitute a quorum to do business; but a smaller number may adjourn from day to day, and may be authorized to compel the attendance of absent members, in such manner, and under such penalties as each house may provide.

Article 21 – Rules

1. The Senate and the People's Assembly shall choose their chairs, their committees, and shall formulate their own procedural rules. Their procedural rules shall not incorporate, accommodate, or otherwise recognize factions or political parties.

2. When seats in the Senate or the People's Assembly from any Member become vacant, the executive authority of the Member shall issue writs of election to fill such vacancies.

3. Each house may punish its members for disorderly behaviour, and, with the concurrence of two thirds, expel a member.

4. Neither house, during the session of the General Assembly, shall, without the consent of the other, adjourn for more than three days, nor to any other place than that in which the two houses shall be sitting.

Article 22 – Committees

The General Assembly may establish such committees and subsidiary organs as it deems necessary for the performance of its functions.

CHAPTER V: THE SECURITY COUNCIL

Article 23 - Composition

1. The Security Council shall consist of fifteen Members of the United Nations, due regard being specially paid, in the first instance to the contribution of Members of the United Nations to the maintenance of international peace and security and to the other purposes of the United Nations, and also to equitable geographical distribution.

    a. The General Assembly shall appoint seven Members of the United Nations to the Security Council, by majority vote of both houses. Members of the Security Council appointed by the General Assembly shall have a seven-year term.

    b. The Secretary-General shall appoint five Members of the United Nations to the Security Council. The term of the Members of the Security Council appointed by the Secretary-General shall be co-terminus with the term of the Secretary-General.

    c. The Council of Philosophers and Scientists shall appoint three Members of the United Nations to the Security Council. Members of the Security Council appointed by the Council of Philosophers and Scientists shall have a fourteen-year term.

2. Vacancies must be filled by the appointing bodies, but only for the remaining duration of the seat's term. No Member can be re-appointed to successive terms on the Security Council.

3. Each member of the Security Council shall have one representative.

Article 24 – Functions and Powers

1. The United Nations shall not have a standing military. It shall conduct military operations, if any, using the militaries of its Members, under the direction of the Security Council. Further, Members shall destroy any biological, chemical, or nuclear weapons, or similar weapons of mass destruction in their possession, and shall not manufacture, possess, or station biological,

chemical, or nuclear weapons, or similar weapons of mass destruction.[8]

2. The Security Council is vested with the authority to maintain international peace and security. Members agree that in carrying out its duties under this responsibility the Security Council acts on their behalf.

3. In discharging these duties the Security Council shall act in accordance with the Purposes and Principles of the United Nations. The specific powers granted to the Security Council for the discharge of these duties are laid down in Chapters VI, VII, VIII, and XII.

4. Any intelligence agency formed under the United Nations shall operate subject to the joint authority of the Security Council and the Secretary-General. Any intelligence agency's meetings shall be open to the public, and its records shall be published electronically, unless otherwise provided by law. No law shall hinder the right of the Security Council and the Secretary-General to attend any meeting of any intelligence agency, to obtain copies of any record of any intelligence

---

[8] From the Rapacki Plan (October 1957).

agency, or to disclose any portion of said records or meetings to the General Assembly.

5. The Security Council shall submit annual and, when necessary, special reports to the General Assembly for its consideration.

Article 25 – Members Bound

1. The Members of the United Nations are bound by the decisions of the Security Council in accordance with the present Charter.

2. The Security Council shall furnish information to and assist the Economic and Social Council, and the Council of Philosophers and Scientists, upon their request.

Article 26 – Powers

In order to promote the establishment and maintenance of international peace and security with the least diversion of the world's human and economic resources to armaments, the Security Council shall have the following powers:

1. With the assistance of the Military Staff Committee referred to in Article 47, to develop and implement a system for the regulation of armaments, which shall share

among the Members the burden of developing and manufacturing only those armaments and armed forces necessary to maintain international peace and security, and shall limit the amount of armaments held by Members to only those necessary and proper for that purpose. The Security Council may address specific armaments in its system for the regulation of armaments.[9]

2. Members shall annually report all armaments and facilities for developing and manufacturing armaments to the Security Council. Any Member that objects to the Security Council's system for the regulation of armaments may appeal to the Secretary-General, who may recommend changes, which may be implemented by a majority of both houses of the General Assembly. Any Member that fails to adequately report all armaments and facilities for developing and manufacturing armaments to the Security Council, or fails to adequately implement the Security Council's system for the

---

[9] Article 8 of the League of Nations Covenant requires reducing arms "to the lowest point consistent with national safety and the enforcement of common action of international obligations."

regulation of armaments, is subject to sanction, suspension, and expulsion, as set forth in this Charter.

3. To order Members to cease any military operation;

4. To order Members to close military bases or installations in the territory of other Members;

5. To commence joint international non-military operations in accordance with Article 41, and international military operations in accordance with Article 42, including the power to order Members to commit military resources to an international conflict, provided that the objective of the military operation is clearly stated in the order, and that the operation will cease once the objective is either achieved or abandoned, and the power to direct and coordinate the military resources of Members participating in international military operations;

6. To commence joint military operations to prevent human rights abuses such as genocide or ethnic cleansing, including the power to order Members to commit military

resources to such conflict pursuant to Article 42, provided that the objective of the military operation is clearly stated in the order, and that the operation will cease once the objective is either achieved or abandoned, and the power to direct and coordinate the military resources of Members participating in military operations;

7. These powers are limited by Section 12.2 hereto.

Article 27 – Voting

1. Each member of the Security Council shall have one vote.

2. Decisions of the Security Council on procedural matters shall be made by an affirmative vote of a simple majority of its Members, except for the recommendation of international military intervention pursuant to Article 42, which shall be made by an affirmative vote of two-thirds of its Members.

3. In decisions under Chapter VI, and under paragraph 3 of Article 52, a party to a dispute shall abstain from voting.

Article 28 – Procedure

1. The Security Council shall be so organized as to be able to function continuously. Each member of the Security Council shall for this purpose be represented at all times at the seat of the United Nations.

2. The Security Council shall hold periodic meetings at which each of its members may, if it so desires, be represented by a member of the government or by some other specially designated representative.

3. The Security Council may hold meetings at such places other than the seat of the United Nations as in its judgment will best facilitate its work.

Article 29 – Subsidiary Organs

The Security Council may establish such subsidiary organs as it deems necessary for the performance of its functions.

Article 30 – Rules

The Security Council shall adopt its own rules of procedure, including the method of selecting its President.

Article 31 – Members Affected

Any Member of the United Nations which is not a member of the Security Council may participate, without vote, in the discussion of any question brought before the Security Council whenever the latter considers that the interests of that Member are specially affected.

Article 32 – Non-Members

Any Member of the United Nations which is not a member of the Security Council or any state which is not a Member of the United Nations, if it is a party to a dispute under consideration by the Security Council, shall be invited to participate, without vote, in the discussion relating to the dispute. The Security Council shall lay down such conditions as it deems just for the participation of a state which is not a Member of the United Nations.

CHAPTER VI: PACIFIC SETTLEMENT OF DISPUTES

Article 33 – First Solution

1. The parties to any dispute, the continuance of which is likely to endanger the maintenance of international peace and security, shall, first of all,

seek a solution by negotiation, enquiry, mediation, conciliation, arbitration, judicial settlement, resort to regional agencies or arrangements, or other peaceful means of their own choice.

2. The Security Council shall, when it deems necessary, call upon the parties to settle their dispute by such means. Parties so called shall participate in such proceedings in good faith.

Article 34 – Investigation

The Security Council may investigate any dispute, or any situation which might lead to international friction or give rise to international or intra-national military conflict, or human rights abuses such as genocide or ethnic cleansing, in order to determine whether the continuance of the dispute or situation is likely to endanger the maintenance of international peace and security, or lead to human rights abuses.

Article 35 – Referrals

1. Any Member of the United Nations may bring any dispute, or any situation of the nature referred to in Article 34, to the attention of the Security Council or of the General Assembly.

2. A state which is not a Member of the United Nations may bring to the attention of the Security

Council or of the General Assembly any dispute to which it is a party if it accepts in advance, for the purposes of the dispute, the obligations of pacific settlement provided in the present Charter.

3. The proceedings of the General Assembly in respect of matters brought to its attention under this Article will be subject to the provisions of Articles 11 and 12.

Article 36 – Recommendations

1. The Security Council may, at any stage of a dispute of the nature referred to in Article 33 or of a situation of like nature, recommend appropriate procedures or methods of adjustment.

2. The Security Council should take into consideration any procedures for the settlement of the dispute which have already been adopted by the parties.

3. In making recommendations under this Article the Security Council should also take into consideration that legal disputes should as a general rule be referred by the parties to the International Court of Justice in accordance with the provisions of the Statute of the Court.

Article 37 – Failure of Pacific Settlement

1. Should the parties to a dispute of the nature referred to in Article 33 fail to settle it by the means indicated in that Article, they shall refer it to the Security Council. Any Member that fails to settle a dispute by the means indicated in Article 33 may be suspended by the General Assembly upon the recommendation of the Security Council, and ratified by the Secretary-General, in accordance with Article 6.

2. If the Security Council deems that the continuance of the dispute is in fact likely to endanger the maintenance of international peace and security, it shall decide whether to take action under Chapter VII or to recommend such terms of settlement as it may consider appropriate.

Article 38 – Further Recommendations

Without prejudice to the provisions of Articles 33 through 37, the Security Council may, if all the parties to any dispute so request, make recommendations to the parties with a view to a pacific settlement of the dispute.

CHAPTER VII: INTERNATIONAL MILITARY INTERVENTION

Article 39 – Initial Determination

The Security Council shall determine the existence of any threat to the peace, breach of the peace, act of aggression, or human rights abuse such as genocide or ethnic cleansing, and shall make recommendations, or decide what measures shall be taken in accordance with Articles 41 and 42, to maintain or restore international peace and security, and prevent human rights abuses.

Article 40 – Provisional Measures

In order to prevent an aggravation of the situation, the Security Council may, before making the recommendations or deciding upon the measures provided for in Article 39, call upon the parties concerned to comply with such provisional measures as it deems necessary or desirable. Such provisional measures shall be without prejudice to the rights, claims, or position of the parties concerned. The Security Council shall duly take account of compliance or failure to comply with such provisional measures.

Article 41 – Non-Military Measures

1. The Security Council may recommend what non-military measures are to be employed. These may include, without limitation, complete or partial interruption of economic relations and of rail, sea, air, postal, telegraphic, radio, satellite, internet, and other means of communication, and the severance of diplomatic relations.

2. The General Assembly shall consider the Security Council's non-military recommendation, and if upon vote of a majority of both houses, shall authorize the Security Council's non-military recommendation. The General Assembly may alter the Security Council's non-military recommendation.

Article 42 – Military Measures

1. The Security Council may determine the means and method that a dispute will be resolved by the Members' militaries if it determines that either: (a) measures provided for in Article 41 would be, or have proved to be inadequate, or (b) that parties to a dispute of the nature referred to in Article 33 or Article 41, have failed to settle it by the means indicated in that Article, or (c) that that the continuance of the dispute is in fact likely to endanger the maintenance of international

Global Governance

peace and security, or cause human rights abuses such as genocide or ethnic cleansing.

2. If the Security Council makes a determination pursuant to Article 42(1), it shall recommend to the General Assembly the means, methods, terms, and objectives of international military intervention.

3. The General Assembly shall consider the Security Council's military recommendation, and if upon vote of two-thirds majority of each house, shall authorize the Security Council's military recommendation. The General Assembly shall have no jurisdiction to alter the Security Council's military recommendation.

4. If the Secretary-General determines that an emergency exits, the Secretary-General may authorize the Security Council's military recommendation, whereupon the General Assembly shall either confirm or un-authorize the Security Council's military recommendation in its regular session, by two-thirds majority vote. If the General Assembly fails to either confirm or un-authorize emergency military action, the Secretary-General's authorization shall remain in force. If the Secretary-General determines that an emergency exits, the Secretary-General may also call a special session of the General Assembly to

consider the Security Council's military recommendation. The Secretary-General shall have no jurisdiction to alter the Security Council's military recommendation, unless the emergency involves genocide or ethnic cleansing.

5. The Security Council's military recommendation, once authorized by the General Assembly pursuant to Section 42(3) or the Secretary-General pursuant to Section 42(4), is binding on all members of the United Nations. Thereafter, the Security Council shall have jurisdiction to enforce the military recommendation, until the purpose of the military intervention has been accomplished, as determined by the International Court of Justice, or the authorization has been revoked by a two-thirds vote of the General Assembly.

6. Any authorization for military action can be revoked or nullified by unanimous vote of the Council of Philosophers and Scientists.

Article 43 – Member Militaries

1. All Members of the United Nations, in order to contribute to the maintenance of international peace and security, shall make available to the Security Council, on its directive, or in accordance with a special agreement or agreements,

armaments, armed forces, assistance, and facilities including logistical, transportation infrastructure, communication infrastructure, and rights of passage, necessary for the purpose of maintaining international peace and security.

2. Special agreement or agreements may govern the numbers and types of forces, their degree of readiness and general location, and the nature of the facilities and assistance to be provided, so long as they conform with the Security Council's system for the regulation of armaments, and Chapter VIII hereto.

3. The agreement or agreements shall be concluded between the Security Council and Members or between the Security Council and groups of Members and shall be subject to ratification by the signatory states in accordance with their respective constitutional processes.

Article 44 – Members Called to Arms

When the General Assembly or Secretary-General has authorized the Security Council's recommendation to use military action, the Security Council shall, before calling upon a Member not represented on it to provide armed forces in fulfilment of the obligations assumed under Article 42 or Article 43, invite that Member, if the Member so desires, to participate in the decisions of the Security Council concerning the employment of contingents of that Member's armed forces.

Article 45 – Immediate Availability

In order to enable the United Nations to take urgent military measures, Members shall make their national military forces immediately available for combined international enforcement action. The strength and degree of readiness of these contingents and plans for their combined action shall be determined within the limits laid down in the special agreement or agreements referred to in Article 43, and by the Security Council with the assistance of the Military Staff Committee.

Article 46 – Planning

Plans for the application of military force shall be made by the Security Council with the assistance of the Military Staff Committee, in accordance with Article 42.

Article 47 – Military Staff Committee

1. There shall be established a Military Staff Committee to advise and assist the Security Council on all questions relating to the Security Council's military requirements for the maintenance of international peace and security, the employment

and command of forces placed at its disposal, the regulation of armaments, and possible disarmament.

2. The Military Staff Committee shall consist of the Chiefs of Staff of the members of the Security Council or their representatives. Any Member of the United Nations not represented on the Committee shall be invited by the Committee to be associated with it when the efficient discharge of the Committee's responsibilities requires the participation of that Member in its work.

3. The Military Staff Committee shall make recommendations to the Security Council for the strategic direction of armed forces placed at the disposal of the Security Council. Questions relating to the command of such forces shall be worked out subsequently.

4. The Military Staff Committee, with the authorization of the Security Council and after consultation with appropriate regional agencies, may establish regional sub-committees. The Military Staff Committee, and all of its sub-committees, shall be under the direct supervision of the Security Council.

Article 48 – Directives

1. While the Security Council's Section 42 recommendation is authorized, Members of the United Nations shall comply with the Security Council's directives in accordance with the authorization. Members shall have no obligation to comply with a Security Council directive that is not authorized.

2. Such directives may be carried out by Member's international agencies.

3. Should any Member dispute any direction by the Security Council, it shall first appeal that decision to the President of the Security Council then, if not satisfied, to the Secretary-General, who may modify the direction, as applied to the disputing Member.

4. Any member that does not substantially comply with a military directive of the Security Council is subject to sanctions, suspension, or expulsion in accordance with this Charter. Should a Member not substantially comply with a military directive of the Security Council, the Security Council shall refer the matter to the General Assembly, to consider whether sanctions or suspension are appropriate.

Global Governance

Article 49 – Mutual Assistance

The Members of the United Nations shall join in affording mutual assistance in carrying out the measures decided upon by the Security Council.

Article 50 – Economic Impact

If military or non-military measures against any state are taken by the United Nations, any other state, whether a Member of the United Nations or not, which finds itself confronted with special economic problems arising from the carrying out of those measures shall have the right to consult the Security Council and the Secretary-General with regard to a solution of those problems.

Article 51 – Self-Defense

Nothing in the present Charter shall impair the inherent right of self-defense if an armed attack occurs against a Member of the United Nations, until the Security Council has taken jurisdiction pursuant to this Charter. Measures taken by Members in the exercise of this right of self-defense shall be immediately reported to the Security Council and shall not in any way affect the authority and responsibility of the Security Council under the present Charter to take at any time such action as it deems necessary in order to maintain or restore international peace and security.

CHAPTER VIII: REGIONAL MILITARY AGREEMENTS

Article 52 – Formation and Enforcement

1. Nothing in the present Charter precludes the formation or existence of regional agreements for military cooperation, which agreements may also form agencies for dealing with matters relating to the maintenance of international peace and security, as are appropriate for regional action. Such regional agreements shall conform with the Security Council's **system for the regulation of armaments, and** are subject to the jurisdiction of the United Nations in accordance with this Charter.

2. The Security Council has jurisdiction to enforce regional military agreements, including the power to enjoin. The Members of the United Nations that have entered, or desire to enter into such regional military agreements, shall submit the agreement to the Security Council, which will make recommendations, which the Members to

the agreement may adopt. The Security Council will submit the amended agreement, along with its recommendations, to the General Assembly, for ratification. Any regional military agreement that has not been ratified by the General Assembly is void and unenforceable. This applies to regional military agreements existing as of the date of this Charter, which shall remain in force until the General Assembly either ratifies the agreement, or votes to reject the agreement.

3. Members of the United Nations that are parties to regional military agreements shall report local disputes falling under the agreement to the Security Council. If the Security Council takes jurisdiction of the local dispute pursuant to Chapter VII, the regional agreement is subject to the Security Council's directives, with respect to the local dispute.

4. This Article in no way impairs the application of Articles 34, 35, 41, and 42.

Article 53 – Use

1. The Security Council shall, where appropriate, utilize such regional military agreements or agencies for enforcement action under its authority. But no enforcement action shall be taken under regional arrangements or by regional

agencies without the authorization pursuant to this Charter.

2. Members who desire to initialize military action pursuant to such regional military agreements shall seek authorization from the United Nations prior to commencing military action. The United Nations may authorize such military action, pursuant to Article 42 hereto. Such authorization may be revoked pursuant to this Charter.

Article 54 – Reporting

Members participating in such regional military agreements shall keep the Security Council fully informed all times of activities undertaken or in contemplation under regional military arrangements or by regional agencies for the maintenance of international peace and security.

CHAPTER IX: REGIONAL ECONOMIC AND SOCIAL AGREEMENTS

Article 55 – Principles

With a view to the creation of conditions of stability and well-being which are necessary for peaceful and friendly relations among nations based on respect for the principle of equal rights and self-determination of peoples, the United Nations shall promote:

a. higher standards of living for all people and full employment for all adults, and conditions of economic and social progress and development necessary to improve standards of living;

b. solutions of international economic, social, health, and related problems; and international cultural and educational cooperation; and

c. universal respect for, and observance of, human rights and fundamental freedoms for all without distinction as to gender, race, religion, sexual preference, sexual expression, age, ethnic origin, or national origin.

Article 56 – Formation and Ratification

1. Nothing in the present Charter precludes the formation or existence of regional economic agreements, which agreements may also form agencies for dealing with matters relating to economic progress, as are appropriate for regional action.

Such regional agreements are subject to the jurisdiction of the United Nations in accordance with this Charter.

2. The Members of the United Nations who have or desire to enter into such regional economic agreements shall submit the agreement to the Economic and Social Council, which will make recommendations, which the Members to the agreement may adopt. The Economic and Social Council will submit the amended agreement, along with its recommendations, to the General Assembly, for ratification. Any regional economic agreement that has not been ratified by the General Assembly is void and unenforceable. This applies to regional economic agreements existing as of the date of this Charter, which shall remain in force until the General Assembly either ratifies the agreement, or votes to reject an amended agreement. Said agreements shall assure that claimants have substantive due process of law.

3. No regional economic agreement shall subvert the authority of the United Nations under this Charter, or the sovereignty of any Member, including Members who are parties to said agreements.

Global Governance

Article 57 – Specialized Agencies

1. The various specialized agencies and non-governmental organizations, including the Bretton Woods organizations, established by intergovernmental agreement and having wide international responsibilities, as defined in their basic instruments, in economic, social, cultural, educational, health, and related fields (referred to herein as specialized agencies), shall be brought into relationship with the United Nations on terms agreeable to the United Nations and each specialized agency.

2. Within five years of the date hereof, the Economic and Social Council shall conduct a review of the specialized agencies, including a review of their charter, their operations, their budgets, and interview their staff, and shall recommend to the Secretary-General the conditions which each would be brought into the United Nations. The Secretary-General shall negotiate these terms with the specialized agencies and, if there is agreement, the specialized agencies shall be brought in to the United Nations.

3. The United Nations may still maintain amicable working relations with specialized agencies not brought in to the United Nations, and nothing

shall preclude them from being brought in to the United Nations in the future.

Article 58 – Co-ordinating Specialized Agencies

The Economic and Social Council shall co-ordinate the policies and activities of the specialized agencies within and without the United Nations.

Article 59 – Creating Specialized Agencies

The United Nations shall, where appropriate, initiate negotiations among the Member states concerned for the creation of any new specialized agencies required for the accomplishment of the purposes set forth in Article 55.

Article 60 – Vesting

Responsibility for the discharge of the functions of the United Nations set forth in this Chapter shall be vested in the General Assembly and, under the authority of the General Assembly, in the Economic and Social Council, which shall have for this purpose the powers set forth in Chapter X.

CHAPTER X: THE ECONOMIC AND SOCIAL COUNCIL

Article 61 - Composition

1. The Economic and Social Council shall consist of forty-two Members of the United Nations. Twenty-one members shall be appointed by the General Assembly. Fourteen members shall be appointed by the Secretary-General. Seven Members shall be appointed by the Council of Philosophers and Scientists.

2. Members of the Economic and Social Council shall have a term of three years, with one third of the seats being re-appointed each year, designated as terms A, B, and C. A retiring member shall be eligible for immediate re-appointment.

3. The General Assembly shall designate their appointees evenly among term A, B, or C. The Secretary-General shall appoint five Members to term A, five Members to term B, and four members to term C. The Council of Philosophers shall appoint two Members to term A, two Members to term B, and three Members to term C. The first class of term A shall have a term of nine years. The first class of term B shall have a term of six years.

4. Each Member of the Economic and Social Council shall have one representative.

Article 62 – Functions and Powers

1. The Economic and Social Council has jurisdiction to enforce regional economic agreements, including the power to enjoin.

2. To be recognized as the legal owner of any property in the United Nations, the owner shall annually report its existence and estimated value, in the form and manner determined by the Economic and Social Council. Custodians of others' economic assets shall report the existence, value, and ownership of economic assets in their custody to the Economic and Social Council.

3. The Economic and Social Council can and shall compel Members, financial institutions, legal entities, persons, and other entities which own or control economic assets, to report the existence, value, and ownership of economic assets. Members, financial institutions, legal entities, persons, and other entities which own or control economic assets can first appeal directions of the Economic and Social Council to the Secretary-General, who may recommend modifications to the direction, then to the International Court of Justice.

Global Governance

4. It shall use the data from this report to create an annual cadaster of the wealth of the Members, and transmit the cadaster to the General Assembly. The purpose of the cadaster is to identify and account for significant holdings of global capital, in all its forms.

5. It shall conduct a census of each Member's human population every seven years, collecting, at a minimum, the name, age, place of birth, annual income from labor and capital, and place of residence of each person.

6. It shall, in consultation with the Council of Philosophers and Scientists, formulate the rules and procedures to implement the cadaster and the census, including the definition of capital.

7. It may enjoin the action or inaction of specialized agencies within the United Nations, and to enjoin the action or inaction of Members who are parties to intergovernmental agreements composing said specialized agencies, with respect said intergovernmental agreements.

8. It shall make an annual report to the Secretary-General and the General Assembly with respect to global economic inequality, and other international economic, social, cultural, educational,

health, and related matters, and may make recommendations with respect to any such matters to the General Assembly to the Members of the United Nations, and to the specialized agencies concerned.

9. It shall in its annual report make recommendations for the purpose of promoting social utility and economic justice of the United Nations' policies, and respect for, and observance of, human rights and fundamental freedoms for all.

10. It may prepare draft conventions for submission to the General Assembly, with respect to matters falling within its competence.

11. It may call, in accordance with the rules prescribed by the United Nations, international conferences on matters falling within its competence.

Article 63 – Specialized Agencies

1. The Economic and Social Council may enter into agreements with any of the specialized agencies referred to in Article 57, defining the terms on which the agency concerned shall be brought into relationship with the United Nations. Such agreements shall be subject to approval by the General Assembly.

2. It may co-ordinate the activities of the specialized agencies through consultation with and recommendations to such agencies and through recommendations to the General Assembly and to the Members of the United Nations.

Article 64 – Reports

1. The Economic and Social Council may compel the specialized agencies within the United Nations to make regular reports. It may make arrangements with the Members of the United Nations and with the specialized agencies within the United Nations to obtain reports on the steps taken to give effect to its own recommendations and to recommendations on matters falling within its competence made by the General Assembly.

2. It may communicate its observations on these reports to the General Assembly.

Article 65 – Members Bound

1. The Members of the United Nations are bound by the decisions of the Economic and Social Council in accordance with the present Charter.

2. The Economic and Social Council may furnish information to the Security Council and shall assist the Security Council upon its request.

Article 66 – Enforcement Functions

1. The Economic and Social Council has jurisdiction to enforce laws of the United Nations designated by the General Assembly to fall under the Economic and Social Council's jurisdiction,

2. It may, with the approval of the General Assembly, perform services at the request of Members of the United Nations and at the request of specialized agencies.

3. It shall perform such other functions as are specified elsewhere in the present Charter or as may be assigned to it by the General Assembly.

Article 67 – Voting

1. Each member of the Economic and Social Council shall have one vote.

2. Decisions of the Economic and Social Council shall be made by a majority of the members present and voting.

Article 68 – Commissions

The Economic and Social Council shall set up commissions in economic and social fields and for the promotion of economic justice, human rights, and such other commissions as may be required for the performance of its functions.

Article 69 – Members Affected

The Economic and Social Council shall invite any Member of the United Nations to participate, without vote, in its deliberations on any matter of particular concern to that Member.

Article 70 – Specialized Agencies Within the United Nations

The Economic and Social Council may make arrangements for representatives of the specialized agencies within the United Nations to participate, without vote, in its deliberations and in those of the commissions established by it, and for its representatives to participate in the deliberations of the specialized agencies.

Article 71 – Specialized Agencies Without the United Nations

The Economic and Social Council may make suitable arrangements for consultation with specialized agencies outside the United Nations, which are concerned with matters within its competence. Such arrangements may be made with international organizations and, where appropriate, with national organizations after consultation with the Member of the United Nations concerned.

Article 72 – Rules

1. The Economic and Social Council shall adopt its own rules of procedure, including the method of selecting its President.

2. The Economic and Social Council shall meet as required in accordance with its rules, which shall include provision for the convening of meetings on the request of a majority of its members.

CHAPTER XI: DECLARATION REGARDING COLONIES AND INDIGENOUS PERSONS[10]

Article 73 – Colonies

1. Self-government is paramount. The United Nations recognizes the competing interests of peoples' self-government, and Members' sovereignty. Any conflict arising between these interests shall be resolved in favor of

---

[10] There are currently sixteen colonies, mostly held by England and the U.S. The UN has declared the intention to establish home rule.

Global Governance

international peace, social and economic justice, and social utility.

2. The members shall annually report to the Secretary-General the status of all colonies under their jurisdiction. If any group of persons disputes their inclusion or exclusion from said report, they shall notify the Secretary-General, who may compel the member to comment and provide evidence regarding the inclusion or exclusion.

3. Members shall, within five years hereof, develop institutions and processes necessary for home rule, including legislative, executive, and judicial institutions, as well as any necessary military capability necessary to further international peace and security, and the colony shall have realized home rule and have fulfilled all conditions precedent to admission to the United Nations, or the Member shall automatically cede all sovereignty over the colony, upon notice by the United Nations pursuant to Section 3;

4. During the five-year transition period referenced in Section 1, Members extract no economic benefit from said colony, except

that which is necessary to fund the development of the institutions and processes necessary for home rule;

5. The General Assembly may, by special or general law, address the independence, self-government, and home rule of colonies. If, after the five-year transition period referenced in Section 3, the General Assembly determines that a colony is capable of home rule, the Secretary-General shall give the colonizing Member notice, and shall be empowered to enforce home rule. If the General Assembly determines that such a colony is, at the end of the five-year transition period referenced in Section 1, still incapable of home rule, it may, by special law, place the colony under the jurisdiction of the International Space and Maritime Commission.

6. For purposes of this Charter, a colony is a geographically contiguous territory over which a Member asserts sovereignty, under which the inhabitants do not have equal rights as other inhabitants, and do not have a full measure of self-government, whether or not the Member has declared the territory as a colony pursuant to this Charter, as determined in accordance with Article

73(1). Self-government is independent home rule, with all sovereign rights.

7. Should a colony that is without self-government wish to establish home rule, duly appointed representatives of the colony may petition the Secretary-General, who may convene a joint session of the Security Council, Economic and Social Council, and Council of Philosophers and Scientists to consider the petition. The Secretary-General shall chair the proceedings. The joint session shall consider evidence given by all interested and affected parties, as well as have the authority to commission its own studies of the petition. The joint session shall make written recommendations, which the Secretary-General shall transmit to the General Assembly, which shall be adopted on majority vote of both houses.

Article 74 – Indigenous People

1. The United Nations recognizes the rights of indigenous peoples located within and across its members' borders. These are groups of people whose presence predated the Member, and who may or may not interact culturally with the Member's population. Indigenous people have the

right to be free from cultural hegemony, the right to occupied lands, and the right to levels of self-determination that are consistent with free people. Members shall defend the rights of indigenous people.

CHAPTER XII: COUNCIL OF PHILOSOPHERS AND SCIENTISTS

Article 75 – Composition

1. The Council of Philosophers and Scientists shall consist of twenty-one members serving terms limited by the shorter of seven years, the member resigning, dying or becoming otherwise incapacitated, or by impeachment and trial. **The initial council shall be nominated by the Secretary-General and confirmed by the General Assembly. Thereafter, when a vacancy occurs, the council shall nominate and confirm its own members, according to its own rules.**

2. To be eligible for the Council of Philosophers and Scientists, a person must be recognized by peers as a leader in a field of science, philosophy, or economics, have integrity, and professional and

moral rigor. Unless waived by a two-thirds majority of the existing council, no member shall have served elected public office.

3. Members shall receive shall receive a salary for their services, to be ascertained by law, and paid out of the treasury of the United Nations.

4. The council can impeach a member for high crimes and abuse of office, or for conduct deemed disqualifying, by majority vote of the non-accused members. Once impeached, the member can be removed from office on trial and conviction by the International Court of Justice, presided by the Chief Judge.

Article 76 – Powers

1. The Council of Philosophers and Scientists has the power to study and declare the social utility of any action of the United Nations.

2. It shall review bills proposed by the General Assembly pursuant to Article 9.4(2) and assign to each bill a social utility rating between positive five and negative five, with positive five being of high social utility, zero being of neutral social utility, and negative five being of negative social utility.

3. It shall assign the social utility rating to a bill within ten days of presentment by the General Assembly. If the Council of Philosophers and Scientists desires more time to study the bill, it shall notify the presenting house how much more time it requires, and the reasons therefor. The presenting house may approve or modify the request by majority vote.

4. It shall have the authority to retain economists and other experts to review the social utility of any action of the United Nations.

CHAPTER XII: WORLD CENTRAL RESERVE BANK

Article 77 – Composition

1. The World Central Reserve Bank is hereby created, which shall be the central bank for all Members of the United Nations. The purpose of the World Central Reserve Bank is to maximize the social utility of monetary policy, to promote global economic justice, and to control global economic inequality.

Global Governance

2. It shall consist of a board of seven governors serving terms limited by the shorter of seven years, or the governor resigning, dying or becoming otherwise incapacitated, or by impeachment and trial. Board members shall be nominated by the Economic and Social Council, and confirmed by the General Assembly.

3. To be eligible for the board of governors of the World Central Reserve Bank, a person must have integrity, and professional and moral rigor. Unless waived by a two-thirds majority of the existing board, no governor shall have served elected public office.

4. Governors shall receive shall receive a salary for their services, to be ascertained by law, and paid out of the treasury of the United Nations.

5. The board of governors can impeach a governor for high crimes and abuse of office. Once impeached, the governor can be removed from office on trial and conviction by the International Court of Justice, presided by the Chief Judge.

Article 78 – Functions

1. The initial board of governors of the World Central Reserve Bank shall draft a charter, consistent with this Charter, and present it to the

General Assembly for approval. Thereon, the World Central Reserve Bank Charter can be amended only by the positive vote of five governors, and ratified by majority vote of the General Assembly. Once ratified by the General Assembly, the charter of the World Central Reserve Bank is binding on all Members.

2. The board of governors can issue a global currency, as provided by law, and can increase or decrease the money supply in order to maintain economic stability, giving due consideration to its primary obligations to promote global economic justice, and to control global economic inequality.

3. The Members shall be the sole shareholders of the World Central Reserve Bank. They shall be offered shares in proportion of their gross domestic product to the world gross domestic product. Should any Member decline to purchase shares, their unpurchased share shall be offered to the other Members, proportionally.

4. The World Central Reserve Bank's records shall be publicly available. The board of governors shall conduct an independent third-party audit of the World Central Reserve Bank every seven years, which shall also be publicly available.

CHAPTER XIV: THE INTERNATIONAL COURT OF JUSTICE[11]

Article 79 – Composition

1. The judicial power of the United Nations shall be vested in the International Court of Justice, and in such inferior courts as the General Assembly may from time to time ordain and establish.

2. There shall be fifteen judges on the International Court of Justice, nominated by the Secretary-General and confirmed by two-thirds of the Senate. Judges of inferior courts are likewise nominated by the Secretary-General and confirmed by two-thirds of the Senate.

3. The judges, both of the International Court of Justice and inferior courts, shall hold their offices during good behavior, and shall, at stated times, receive for their services, a compensation, which shall not be diminished during their continuance in office.

---

[11] Deleted two chapters regarding trusteeship council, as it has fulfilled its mission and ceased operation.

4. A judge of the International Court of Justice, or any inferior court, can be impeached by the People's Assembly for high crimes and abuse of office. Once impeached, the judge can be removed from office on trial and conviction by the Senate, presided by the Chief Judge of the International Court of Justice, unless the judge is a member of the International Court of Justice, in which case the President of the Council of Philosophers and Scientists shall preside.

Article 80 – Powers

1. The judicial Power shall extend to all cases and controversies, in law and equity, arising under this Charter and the Universal Declaration of Human Rights, the laws of the United Nations, and agreements made, or which shall be made, under their authority; to all cases affecting ambassadors, other public ministers and consuls; to all cases of admiralty and maritime jurisdiction; to all cases involving the United Nation's sovereign jurisdiction, such as colonies, international waters, Antarctica, and outer space; to controversies to which the United Nations shall be a party; to controversies between two or more Members; between citizens of different Member states, and between a Member state, or the citizens thereof, and foreign states, citizens or subjects.

Global Governance

2. The judicial power shall extend to the determination of whether the laws of the United Nations, and executive interpretations thereof, comply with this Charter. Any Member, or citizen of a Member, shall have standing to make such a challenge, with or without particularized harm.

3. The International Court of Justice has final jurisdiction to hear claims arising from or under said regional economic agreements, and may conduct a *de novo* review of any findings of fact or law, including whether the claimants were given substantive due process of law. The International Court of Justice shall make its own rules regarding review of said claims. The right to review by the International Court of Justice under regional economic agreements is non-waivable.

4. A state which is not a Member of the United Nations may become a party to the Statute of the International Court of Justice on conditions to be determined in each case by the General Assembly upon the recommendation of the Security Council.

5. In all cases affecting ambassadors, other public ministers and consuls, and those in which a Member state shall be party, the International Court of Justice shall have original jurisdiction. in

all the other cases before mentioned, the International Court of Justice shall have appellate jurisdiction, both as to law and fact, with such exceptions, and under such regulations as the General Assembly shall make.

6. The trial of all crimes, except in cases of impeachment, shall be by jury; and such trial shall be held in the Member state where the said crimes shall have been committed; but when not committed within any Member state, the trial shall be at such place or places as the General Assembly may by law have directed.

Article 81 – Members Bound

1. Each Member of the United Nations is bound by the decision of the International Court of Justice in any case to which it is a party.

2. If any party to a case fails to perform the obligations incumbent upon it under a judgment rendered by the International Court of Justice, the Court may impose sanctions, including suspension of a Member state. The General Assembly may expel a Member state suspended by the Court.

Article 82 – Other Tribunals

Unless a right or obligation is non-waivable under this Charter, nothing in the present Charter shall prevent Members of the United Nations from entrusting the solution of their differences to other tribunals by virtue of agreements already in existence or which may be concluded in the future.

Article 83 – Advisory Opinions

1. The General Assembly, the Council of Philosophers and Scientists, the Economic and Social Council, or the Security Council may request the International Court of Justice to give an advisory opinion on any legal question.

2. Other organs of the United Nations and specialized agencies, which may at any time be so authorized by the General Assembly, may also request advisory opinions of the Court on legal questions arising within the scope of their activities.

CHAPTER XV: THE SECRETARIAT

Article 84 – Election

1. The Secretary-General shall be nominated by either the Security Council, the Economic and Social Council, or the Council of Philosophers and Scientists, and elected by a two-thirds vote of both houses of the General Assembly. The Secretary-General is limited to one seven-year term in office.

2. The Secretary-General shall act in that capacity in all meetings of the General Assembly.

3. To be eligible for the office of Secretary-General, a person must be at least thirty-five years of age, and have been a citizen of a Member for at least five years.

4. The Secretary-General shall receive compensation, which shall neither be increased nor diminished during the Secretary-General's term. The Secretary-General shall not receive within that

period any other compensation or emolument from the United Nations, or any Member.[12]

5. If the Secretary-General dies or, as determined by the General Assembly, becomes unable to discharge the duties of office, the chair of the Council of Philosophers and Scientists shall hold the executive power *pro tem*, until such time as the General Assembly can elect a new Secretary-General.

6. The Secretary-General can be impeached by the People's Assembly for high crimes and abuse of office. Once impeached, the Secretary-General can be removed from office on trial and conviction by the Senate, presided by the Chief Judge of the International Court of Justice.

Article 85 – Powers

1. The executive power shall be vested in a Secretary-General of the United Nations.

2. **The Secretary-General** shall have power to grant reprieves and pardons for offences against

---

[12] Based on Art. 2, Sec. 1, Cl. 7 of the U.S. Constitution, which is the basis of my lawsuit against President Trump.

the United Nations, except in cases of impeachment.

3. The Secretary-General shall make an annual report to the General Assembly on the work of the United Nations.

Article 86 – International Peace and Security

The Secretary-General may bring to the attention of the Security Council any matter which may threaten the maintenance of international peace and security.

Article 87 – Performance of Duties

1. In the performance of their duties the Secretary-General and the staff shall not seek or receive instructions from any government or from any other authority external to the United Nations. They shall refrain from any action which might reflect on their position as international officials responsible only to the United Nations.

2. Each Member of the United Nations undertakes to respect the exclusively international character of the responsibilities of the Secretary-General and the staff and not to seek to influence them in the discharge of their responsibilities.

Global Governance

Article 88 – Staffing

1. The staff shall be appointed by the Secretary-General under regulations established by the General Assembly.

2. Appropriate staffs shall be permanently assigned to the Security Council, the Economic and Social Council, the Council of Philosophers and Scientists, and the World Central Reserve Bank, and, as required, to other organs of the United Nations. These staffs shall form a part of the Secretariat.

3. The paramount consideration in the employment of the staff and in the determination of the conditions of service shall be the necessity of securing the highest standards of efficiency, competence, and integrity. Due regard shall be paid to the importance of recruiting the staff on as wide a geographical basis as possible, with proportional representation in the staff by gender, race, religion, sexual preference, sexual expression, age, ethnic origin, or national origin.

4. Recognizing that public corruption undermines the rule of law and the legitimacy of the United Nations, the General-Secretary shall propose a code of ethics for consideration, amendment, and adoption by the General Assembly. The

code of ethics shall make exchanging official actions for personal gain, directly or indirectly, including gain for a family member, an abuse of office, and mandatory grounds for termination of employment or, if the office is held pursuant to this Charter, grounds for impeachment for abuse of office. The code of ethics shall also include a mechanism for restitution and claw-back of monies gained by abuse of office, to the United Nations, and may also provide criminal sanctions for corrupt actions.

Article 89 – International Space and Maritime Commission

1. There shall be created within the Secretariat an International Space and Maritime Commission, which shall consist of fourteen members serving terms limited by the shorter of seven years, or the member resigning, dying or becoming otherwise incapacitated, or by impeachment and trial. **Members of the commission shall be nominated by the Secretary-General and confirmed by the General Assembly.**

2. To be eligible for the International Space and Maritime Commission, a person must be at least twenty-five years old, be a citizen of a Member for at least five years, have integrity, and professional and moral rigor. Unless waived by a two-

thirds majority of the existing commission, no member shall have served elected public office.

3. Members shall receive shall receive a salary for their services, to be ascertained by law, and paid out of the treasury of the United Nations.

4. The commission can impeach a member for high crimes and abuse of office. Once impeached, the member can be removed from office on trial and conviction by the International Court of Justice, presided by the Chief Judge.

Article 90 – ISMC Powers

1. The International Space and Maritime Commission shall administer the United Nations' jurisdiction over colonies, international waters, Antarctica, and outer space.

2. It shall be the United Nations' ambassadorial representative with respect to non-member nations, and extraterrestrial aliens.

CHAPTER XVI: MISCELLANEOUS PROVISIONS

Article 91 – Registry

1. Every treaty and every international agreement entered into by any Member of the United Nations after the present Charter comes into force shall as soon as possible be registered with the Secretariat and published by it.

2. No party to any such treaty or international agreement which has not been registered in accordance with the provisions of paragraph 1 of this Article may invoke that treaty or agreement before any organ of the United Nations.

Article 92 – Charter Prevails

In the event of a conflict between the obligations of the Members of the United Nations under the present Charter and their obligations under any other international agreement, their obligations under the present Charter shall prevail.

Article 93 – Legal Capacity

The United Nations shall enjoy in the territory of each of its Members such legal capacity as may be necessary for the exercise of its functions and the fulfilment of its purposes.

Article 94 – Privileges and Immunities

1. The United Nations shall enjoy in the territory of each of its Members such privileges and immunities as are necessary for the fulfilment of its purposes.

2. Representatives of the Members of the United Nations and officials of the United Nations shall similarly enjoy such privileges and immunities as are necessary for the independent exercise of their functions in connection with the United Nations.

3. The General Assembly may make recommendations with a view to determining the details of the application of paragraphs 1 and 2 of this Article or may propose conventions to the Members of the United Nations for this purpose.

Article 95 – Standard Pitch

The standard pitch shall henceforth be A = 431.4757 hz.

Article 96 – Political Speech

1. Donations to political campaigns by corporations and other legal entities can be regulated by law.

2. Political speech by corporations and other legal entities can be regulated by law.

CHAPTER XVII: NOT USED

CHAPTER XVIII: AMENDMENTS

Article 97 – Adoption and Ratifications

Amendments to the present Charter shall come into force for all Members of the United Nations when they have been adopted by a vote of two thirds of the members of the General Assembly and ratified in accordance with their respective constitutional processes by two thirds of the Members of the United Nations.

Article 98 – Charter Review

1. A General Conference of the Members of the United Nations for the purpose of reviewing the

Charter shall be held the members of the General Assembly every seven years. Each Member of the United Nations shall have one vote in the conference. The Secretary-General, the Security Council, the Economic and Social Council, and the Council of Philosophers and Scientists shall submit recommended Charter amendments for consideration by the General Conference.

2. Any alteration of the present Charter recommended by a two-thirds vote of the conference shall take effect when ratified in accordance with their respective constitutional processes by two thirds of the Members of the United Nations including all the permanent members of the Security Council.

CHAPTER XIX: RATIFICATION AND SIGNATURE

Article 99 – Ratification

1. The present Charter shall come into force when it is ratified by the signatory states in accordance with their respective constitutional processes.

2. The ratifications shall be deposited with United Nations archive, which shall notify all the signa-

tory states of each deposit as well as the Secretary-General of the United Nations when he has been appointed.

3. Ratification of this Charter by a Member is for itself, and on behalf of all persons and legal entities under its jurisdiction, who are also bound hereby,

Article 100 – Signature

The present Charter, of which the Chinese, French, Russian, English, and Spanish texts are equally authentic, shall remain deposited in the United Nations archive. Duly certified copies thereof shall be transmitted by the archivist to the Governments of the other signatory states.

IN FAITH WHEREOF the representatives of the Governments of the United Nations have signed the present Charter. DONE at the city of ____ the ___ day of ____, _____.

www.ingramcontent.com/pod-product-compliance
Lightning Source LLC
Chambersburg PA
CBHW021816170526
45157CB00007B/2612